TALKS WITH A CLASS

TALKS WITH A CLASS

ANNIE BESANT

GYAN

Published by

Gyan Publishing House
5, Ansari Road
Daryaganj, New Delhi-110002
Phone: 011-47034999, 9811692060
E-mail: books@gyanbooks.com

Distribution Network
gyanbooks.com
India, USA, Canada, UK, Australia, France

ISBN: 978-81-212-8674-9 (PB)
First Published, 1922

2nd Impression 2023

Printed at: Gyan Press, Delhi.

TALKS WITH A CLASS
Author: Annie Besant

TALKS WITH A CLASS

TALKS WITH A CLASS

BY

ANNIE BESANT

THEOSOPHICAL PRESS
826 OAKDALE AVENUE, CHICAGO, ILL.
1922

INDEX

CHAPTER I

DEVACHAN—A WORLD OF THOUGHT

We are often asked questions about Devachan, and specific information about it has been given in our books and in our lectures. But if you understand only stray *facts* concerning Devachan, you will really have only fragments of knowledge, for though your immediate question may be answered, it may not help you to deal with your next question. What you want to do, if you are really to get a grasp of the laws of the spiritual world, is to take the underlying *cause,* study it and grasp it. You do not then answer questions by *facts,* but you apply the *principle* that you grasp to explain the facts that you come across. That is the only way really of gaining knowledge worth calling knowledge, because there is no end to facts and therefore no end to questions; but you can answer them yourself if you can only apply their underlying principles.

So with regard to the underlying principle of Devachan. If it is grasped, if you really understand what it means and work it out, you will be able to answer all the subsidiary questions yourselves, instead of bringing them to other people and memorizing, as it were, the answers. The object, you must remember, of all our teaching is not to give facts to memorize, as is done in the case of ordinary knowledge, but to evolve in yourselves the faculties which will enable you to understand and grasp facts and arrange them in their proper place. Of course it is enormously more difficult, but it means growth, whereas the other really only means marking time.

With regard to Devachan, the basic principle is that it is a World of Thought. That is a phrase with which the whole of you are familiar; and if you are asked what Devachan is, you can say: "A world of thought." But if you realize what those three words, "world of thought," mean, you might work out the whole of the devachanic conditions for anyone whose mental possibilities would enable him to undersand it.

You have to realize what it means to be living in the mental body. It does not mean in Devachan something quite different from what it means down here. Only down here you do not realize your life in the mental body, but in the workings of the mental body as transmitted to the physical brain, which is a very different matter. You cut off at each stage a large number of your mental perceptions. It is just like shutting windows as you go down. On the mental level the windows are very, very numerous—practically continuous. As you come down into the astral, a number of those windows are closed; into the physical, nearly all of them are closed. If you did that in thought, if you used your imagination to do it, you would be able to understand practically the devachanic state, and you would give the right meaning to such words as "illusory," and the others which are used in describing it.

Try to think of yourselves without the astral and the physical bodies. You know I have often told you that one of the most useful exercises is to take the physical body as it is, and shut off one of your senses mentally, taking first of all that which effects you the least, and so going on and on until only one sense is left. You will find, if that is then eliminated, the physical world is out of contact with you. H. P. B. was very fond of teaching her pupils to do this. She would say: "Go and meditate as though you were blind." You would shut out your sense of sight, think, as far as you could, as though you had not the sense of sight. It is difficult to do that, because of all the mental impressions that you gained through that sense in the past. That is where the real difficulty comes in. You can shut out the sense of sight by thinking of yourself as in the dark, but it is far more difficult to shut out all that that sense of sight has impressed upon you during the whole of your waking life, and to get back into the condition, say, of the man born blind, who has never seen. I remember trying to do that once in Avenue Road by talking a great deal with people who used to come to the meetings from a blind asylum close by. I made friends with them, and gradually they came to tell me how the world seemed to them. Of course there was an enormous difference between the person who had been born blind, and the person who had seen and could recreate the world around him. But the ideas of the man who had been born blind were very peculiar. His ideas of the world were based on what people said to him about it, and he had to add to their words meanings of his own which they could not convey. Take the idea of color. To convey the idea of color to a man who has been born blind is an almost impossible thing. You have nothing to go upon with it.

In that fashion you can practically learn something at least of how the world seems to these people: then you can imagine this in meditation. Again, a way of getting some ideas on the subject would be to take the biography of Helen Keller, who was practically out of contact with the world, you might say, except by touch. From that you would see what the world was to her, and how it gradually changed with the very beautiful course of instruction through which she was taken.

It is only by this kind of definite, practical effort of the imagination, trained by facts, not allowed to fly all over the place, that you will really gain the power of isolating yourselves from the physical sheath deliberately and consciously. Then you try to do the same thing in the astral world; then observe what you come to in the world of mind alone. You take with you, of course, into that world of mind all the impressions which have been made through the physical and astral bodies. The workings of the mind have been thus focalized, and the result in that manner is not fabricated but is nearer the truth. If you can work that out, not hastily, but slowly and gradually and steadily, you will be able to get a very clear idea of the devachanic state, because all that you have left there is the mental body as a means of contact with the outer world. Hence, of course, as you know perfectly well, the immense importance in your present life of gaining a very great variety of mental impressions, a rich consciousness full of impressions, and above all full of what you have made out of the impressions, which is the real work of thought; not the mere bricks which have been given you from this outer world of senses, but the houses that you construct out of those bricks, because that is done by the building power of mind.

One valuable thing H. P. B. taught us was that you do not jump at things in Occultism: you gradually, bit by bit, build them up. Her idea, for instance, of creating the picture of the Master was very different from the idea of most people when they do it. Of course, I know that if you have a strong power of visualization you can do it very quickly, but even then, if you want the training that she laid so much stress upon, so that every power that you have becomes a tool for your use, you would find her method very helpful. She told us that the way to make a picture of the Master was to begin at the feet and to work up, step by step, as though we had a paint brush in our hands, and paint the picture mentally bit by bit. Not one of the impressionist pictures, because that is not the sort that she wanted us to do. She wanted an accurate picture of the physical thing very, very carefully created. I am not saying that that is the highest form of painting, but I am only telling you what she wanted us to do. If that is done, you may say that it is done once for all; and that you can do by concentrating the mind.

Similarly, when you are trying to realize this mental state, apart from the continual checks that your thoughts receive by the grosser matter of the physical world, which you are not able to affect very strongly by your thought—if you take the pains to do this thoroughly and carefully, you will find that the result is that you get a clear idea of the devachanic state.

There are two points about that which need special notice. One is that there is no check upon it from outside. When you are thinking here in your brain, your thoughts are constantly corrected by outside happenings, and constantly corrected also by the working of the reason from the impressions of the senses, which is a very important factor. The senses convey the *impressions* which they receive from outside; there is no guarantee that those are accurate as regards the *facts*. The senses are perfectly accurate so far as the impression goes of what they get; but the conclusion drawn from that impression is very often entirely wrong, as you know. For example, take the common illustration of the sun rising. You see it rise; there is no doubt that you see it rise. The eye is perfectly accurate in conveying to your brain the impression made upon it. But the conclusion that the sun is moving is, as you know, quite wrong. Hence with every mental impression you get a double action; you come up against certain physical facts that you can't get away from; then by your reason you have to correct the impression they make upon you.

There is nothing of that in Devachan, and that makes an immense difference naturally. Hence the importance of accurate thinking here, if Devachan is to be useful. You must train your imagination not to be controlled by the impressions which physical plane facts make upon your senses. Then in your Devachan you will not have a very mistaken sort of idea of things in general. The use of the physical plane is to make your mental powers precise and accurate, to give them a precision which in their own plane they have not got until the mental powers of that particular person have been subjected to a long amount of training from the physical plane. It is only that which takes away the vagueness, the cloudiness, such as you will find, for instance, in all the inferior ranks of devas.

The devas have the vaguest and cloudiest conceptions of things: very beautiful from the artistic standpoint, exceedingly beautiful, but inaccurate so far as facts are concerned. They don't know the facts; they are not living in the world of physical facts. They have no experience of it except by playing upon it from outside, and they are not corrected by it in any sense. That is one of the reasons why we are told that while a deva friend may be an exceedingly interesting person, you had better be very careful how you follow out his ideas, because he may lead you into the most extraordinary bogs; not only bogs of inaccurate thinking but also bogs of exceedingly immoral conduct, judged by the ordinary standard. That is a danger from the lower order of devas—not, of course, from the higher; they are not in themselves immoral at all in their world, but they are entirely different from us. They have no relation to the facts amidst which humanity is evolving, because, as I think I once explained to you, they see only the end, they don't care one scrap about the means. A certain thing has to be done and they do it. And that is all right in their world. But supposing they tell you to do it; you come up against all the facts of this world, among which there are laws, such as: "Thou shalt not kill." Now the deva's particular business may be to kill at the moment. He cares about nothing except that particular thing which he has to do. But if he used you as an agent, as he is quite willing to do sometimes to save himself trouble, then naturally you come into contact with the forms of human justice. Hence the unwisdom of taking a deva as a guide. I am not speaking about the high Devas, of course, but of most of the devas on the astral plane, the nature-spirits, as we often call them, who are most in contact with human beings. They are very pleasant friends, because they can be very loving creatures, and there is no earthly reason why you should not enjoy their company, provided you realize that the power to make pictures does not necessarily go hand in hand with an understanding of human affairs. As I have sometimes told you, when such a deva occasionally comes into contact with a human being and guides him, that human being becomes a most annoying and troublesome person; very charming, but most troublesome in ordinary human society. You don't know what to do with him or her.

When you come to Devachan, you carry into it just the mental furniture you have—neither less nor more. You should therefore take advantage of your stay in the physical world to make your thinking accurate and precise, because the amount of inaccuracy in people's ordinary talk is something astounding when you begin to analyze it. You had better find it out in yourself first; it always answers to make one's experiments in one's own body. If you try it, you will find out how extraordinarily untruthful you are. I am not being rude, because I found the same thing in myself, though I rather prided myself on being very truthful and accurate. Without thinking, you color things; without thinking, you make a nice story about a thing, a little more or a little less than actually happened, and so on. All those things will very much limit the usefulness of your Devachan, because you will carry with you a whole mass of imaginings and fancies which are not in either heaven or earth. Hence you will not get out of Devachan all you should get, the growth of all experience into faculty, which is one use of Devachan.

That lack of correction, then, by the hard outside experience which you cannot manage, is one thing to think of; and remember that in the mental world matter answers to whatever you think, at once responds and takes shape according to your thought.

The other important point, which you should specially notice with regard to your stay in Devachan, is your inherent shades of perception and your capability to appreciate. That is the other great limit. You know in Devachan everything to which you can answer, and nothing more. You can increase that capacity in Devachan if you started here on any point, but you can't begin a new starting point there. It is not a world of causes: it is a world of effects. Hence the great importance of multiplying, so far as possible, your points of contact with other minds, as well as your points of contact with the outside physical world, so as to get many starting points of new lines of development in Devachan.

Every great mind that you come into touch with is one such germinal capacity for evolution in the devachanic state. Where you begin is the great point, for you will thus make endless opportunities for evolution in Devachan. I think on the whole that the "capability to appreciate" is the most important point as regards the devachanic life. Think for a moment of how very little we can appreciate the Master. We do not know the Master; we know only the impressions that He makes upon us, by which we are able to respond. You come, let us say, in the night-world, in the world when your body is sleeping, into touch with the Master. You feel you are coming into touch with Him, which is perfectly true; but only with a little bit of Him, that fragment in Him to which you are able to answer.

You want to increase your capacity to respond to greatness; and there are two ways, of course—by the expansion of the intellect, and by the expansion of devotion. The expansion of the intellect is the more difficult and slower work. It has to be done, of course: you must not neglect it. The expansion of the heart by love and devotion is comparatively rapid, and the tendency, when you come across anyone who is a good deal greater than yourself, to try to appreciate rather than to criticise, means that you are increasing the part of you which is responsive to that which is beyond your present capacity.

It is not necessary to limit that to persons greater than yourself. One can learn something from every individual one meets, because every Self is unfolding in his own way, not in yours, nor in the way of anybody else. He may be very much less unfolded than you are yourself; but on the other hand, he may have unfolded a particular point that you have not unfolded, and one way of profiting by people around you is by trying to come into touch with them on the point on which you do not sympathize. If you sympathized, that would mean that you had the power to respond; when you do not sympathize, it means that you have not the power to respond to that particular point. That is the simple answer. Instead of thinking of the person: "He is irresponsive, he is uninteresting and very dull" (I dare say he may be), adapt yourself to him, and try to find something in him which you do not appreciate, and which you ought to appreciate.

A witty Frenchwoman once said, when she had been to a party and was asked if she had not found it dull: "It would have been very dull, if I had not been there myself." That is exactly the spirit you want. There is nothing dull in this world for a person who is himself intellectual and responsive; and if he finds it dull, it is because he is lacking in something which he ought to supply.

Everyone who does much in the way of leading, or who has what is called the power of leading, is a person, who, whether he knows it or not, is always learning something from every person he meets. A person may be very dull, stupid, undeveloped, but instinctively the person who is a leader at heart and has the power to lead, will meet that man on the one point that the man knows more about than he does, and he will learn something from him. The attitude of receptivity makes the man open out, and he will explain the best that is in him, and the leader will get that out of him, and so much will be added to his own capacity to respond, while the man will love him.

That is one of the most practical and useful lessons that I know. When you study Occultism you come into it with an understanding as to why you are doing it, which you did not have before, but it is a wonderful thing which is instinctive in a person who has the power to lead. The very fact that he leads means that he is more developed along a certain line than the other people whom he leads consciously. Hence his need to be able to come into contact with very large numbers of people, because he is not effective as a leader if he does not get a big following. Some do this naturally, and I suppose instinctively, but Occultists do it deliberately. With every person whom they meet they say, as it were, to the ego of that person: "What have you got to say to me?" and they do not try to push what they have to say on the other person. They give the other person a chance to explain himself.

If two people happen to meet who are both trying to do this same thing, it may be a little amusing, because each is trying to find out the point on which he does not contact the other. Well, then the stronger wins, and the one who has the more power of assimilation is the one who will get the most out of it. But this deliberate effort is comparatively rare, and if you will really practice it, you will find the world becomes enormously more interesting; you will never find it dull, for the reason that you are always learning something.

That is one of the practices which make Devachan rich. You have developed an enormous number of points of contact with the outer world of thought, and along each of those you can work. That is what makes the Devachan of the developed person who goes there so very long; he must have time to work out all these different things, and his progress is enormous. I think I have said to you before, that there are two sides to that, and that the very, very long Devachan is apt to take a person too much out of touch with the world and thus make him forget it, as it were, so that when he comes back again the world has changed so enormously that there are a great many things in it to which he does not respond, and he has to learn to do so.

You cannot have everything in character and responsiveness at the present time, until you reach perfection—perhaps I won't say perfection—until you reach the Jivanmukta stage.

There is always a certain lopsidedness growing out of our past, and we gradually learn to understand our own lopsidedness.

If you can follow out these lines of thinking, you will be able to answer all the questions put to you on Devachan, and that is the value of it to you. It should help you not only in your own experience at present, but also in helping other people to understand. This clear appreciation of what Devachan means will be found helpful in answering people's questions, which sometimes seem puzzling to you.

It has been said that our ideas in Devachan are of the ego's own making. Do not mistake that, as so many people do, by thinking it less real than what your ego is going through down here, because the whole of your contact with the world here is also of your ego's own making. He cannot alter the facts that he meets that are not his own, so to speak, but he alters his attitude to the facts, and therefore the impression that the facts make on him.

Each one of you in his own world is living quite separate from everybody else in his own world. You only know the impressions that other people make upon you, modified by your own receptivity. You do not know other people. Just because one of them, who may be stronger, can knock you down physically, you think that is real. That does not make him real to you. It only means that down on this physical plane one kind of matter does not readily permeate another, and if one kind bangs up against another, the stronger knocks the weaker down. It is merely that one fact.

You are already living in the world of your own making. That is what I want you to realize. It is not real; it is a world of your own impressions only, and that is what you are living in, and that is why you make so many mistakes, which we all do and have done. It is because we are living in an unreal world among other people, each of whom is living in his own unreal world; it is because we come tumbling up against each other with all our unrealities that we naturally misunderstand each other. If you saw a human being as he is, you would not misunderstand, you would understand him. Then you would never quarrel with him. It is because you see him, not as he is, but as he appears to you, that you have misunderstandings and quarrels and all the rest of it. Unrealities make these, not realities. So you are truly living now in a world of your own making.

In Devachan the difference is that all the disagreeable things are kept out. Of course that makes a great difference in your happiness, but they are artificially kept out, just as artificially as, when you go into your own room, you close the door and thus shut out the outer world.

CHAPTER II

FACTORS IN SPIRITUAL PROGRESS

In our Theosophical studies considerable confusion is caused by the fact that so many different meanings are given to the word "spiritual." Spirituality is the realization of the One, hence of Oneness. Strictly speaking, therefore, that word, when applied to the planes of our system, ought to be confined to the highest planes, the atmic, the buddhic, and the upper manasic, as it becomes illuminated by buddhi—those which are the direct reflections, or rather reproductions, of the Monad. Those are the real, the only, phases which ought, strictly speaking, to be called spiritual, because the Monad himself, the essential Self of each, taking up the atoms of nirvanic, buddhic and manasic matter, holding these and manifesting himself in connection with these, thus gives us the spiritual in our universe. Nothing save that ought strictly speaking, to be called spiritual, and that is the definition that ought to govern our thought when we are trying to be accurate.

In evolution there is the drawing up of the essence of the manasic into the buddhic, the drawing up of both of these into the atmic, and so the reproduction of what is often called the "triple Atma," which was separated off into these three distinct atomic existences in evolution. If you get hold of and keep that general idea very clearly and definitely in mind, it will guide you. The coming forth out of the darkness, the manifestation, or reproduction, and the going back, are the actual course of the Monad. He reproduces himself with his triple nature on the nirvanic plane, then picks up the buddhic and manasic atoms and enfolds himself in those: each aspect of the Monad is represented by what you may call a technically-separated phase during human evolution.

This distinction of the atoms gives a precision that did not exist in the Monadic consciousness on his own plane: that three-faced unity, putting himself outward and taking up this connection with matter, manifests forth as a triplicity, a definitely threefold existence, and that is the Self in the world of men.

If you are fond of the metaphysical way of looking at things, you might almost compare that with the appearance for the long day of Brahma of the Saguna-Brahman, Sachchidananda, where you have distinctly the Divine Triplicity, which is the root of every Trinity in all religions. That coming forth into cosmic manifestation we have reproduced in our solar system by the LOGOS, of whom the Monad is a fragment, and his is made a more distinct process for the purpose of unfolding; he regathers himself up again when the human evolution is over, and the superhuman evolution begins. You have thus that long swing of the opening life from the nirvanic and back to the nirvanic, and between the two is the whole of human evolution. That finishes with the Initiation of the Jivanmukta, the Master, where the superhuman evolution begins.

I remind you of this because to keep the whole of

that clearly in mind through your study is essential to the clarity of your thought. It is the indefiniteness, the confusion, the muddle of thought, which makes so many difficulties for almost all people; and you who are earnest students, ought to get over that, and not have this vague, indefinite, so-called "thinking," that you find normally, but the clear, precise understanding of what this unfolding means, and how this unfolding of the True triple Ego, of the Spirit, of the Self, of him who endures because he is eternal, influences and brings about what we call evolution, the building up of the bodies to suit this gradual unfolding. Everything is in the Self, but each thing comes forth into the outer world very slowly and gradually. That is paralleled, correlated, with ordinary scientific evolution of forms; it controls them, guides them, shapes them, and is the inspiring life.

Realizing that, you will also understand quite clearly and definitely what it means when one of these evolving and developing creatures "falls out of the stream." There you have, not the inspiration of the life of the Self, the third Life-Wave shaping and guiding the forms, but the appropriation by the forms of the life of that higher type, that higher type which ought to purify and redeem matter here, instead of being dragged down and identified with and imprisoned in matter. That is what H. P. B. calls the "second death," though she does not go into detail. What really happens is that the second Life-Wave, which is in all the atoms of the forms, seizes hold of and blends with itself this higher type of life from the third Life-Wave, takes into itself part of that life and, keeping hold of it, weakens this embodied Ray of the Monad; it weakens it by imprisoning in the atoms of the astral and mental bodies part of this monadic Ray, so that it can no longer function in the outer world. It therefore goes back to its source, having lost, not gained, by the manifestation; there is less life there than there was, instead of more, for part of the life has been dragged away from and imprisoned in the forms, and these breaking away from the Ray, carry the living creature into a descending path. The life diminishes with each rebirth, and finally passes back into the animal, vegetable, and mineral kingdoms, and is mixed up in the general reservoir of material to be worked up into later evolutions.

That is the whole of the mystery of the "second death," the "eighth plane," and the other phrases that are used. In such cases the Selves are withdrawn into the plane beyond the nirvanic, and have to wait for a new great cycle of evolution before the Monad can begin a new work. Although this Ray returns less than it went out, it blends again with the life on its own plane; there is no real diminution of life possible. That particular Monad has for the time being lost the unfoldment which he might have gained, but he is one with the great Monadic Host to rebegin the course of unfolding life. That unfolding of the life is necessary for him in order that he may realize his own divinity, and, having become master of matter, become one of the consciously creative forces of future universes.

In the early days, when we did not possess as much knowledge as we now have, and did not have all the present literature, we puzzled over this phrase about the "dropping out," and the passing into the "planet of death," the mental as well as the physical satellite of our earth. The moon is the physical satellite of our earth, and, as you know, we were all on it at one time and came on to our present active planet. That, belonging to a past evolution, is now from a physical standpoint a dead world—a dying world, would perhaps be more strictly accurate.

That physical counterpart has connections on the astral and mental planes—the lower mentality, the two and a half planes which are the changing planes of bodies constantly renewed, the bodies that are formed of them, the constantly-changing bodies that are formed of them. All this has its relation to the moon, and you can therefore realize what is meant in the old writings as to the "eighth sphere," and why people were puzzled as to what this meant. Some thought that the "eighth sphere" was the physical moon, which did not seem an unnatural meaning.

We may think of the moon as we think of our own embodiments, with physical, astral and mental bodies. The moon is a triple body just as we are. Those are the mortal forms; they constitute our mortal body. So with the moon there is a physical, an astral and a mental, all connected with the physical, the astral and the mental of our earth, closely related, and in each case, on their own particular planes of matter, the satellites of the earth.

But we have there not the mental plane as you know it, where Devachan is and where your thought is working, but its corresponding sphere reflected downward as it were. There is the world as we know it, and the denser world which is part of it. As we have our astral, there is a lower astral which is denser than the dense physical, and so also you have the mental reflected down below the lower astral. There is the same correspondence in this that you have in the reflection of a mountain in a lake. The lowest part of the mountain is the highest part of the reflection, and so you look downward and downward until the apex of the mountain is the deepest point in the water—the law of reflection, of course—a perfect analogy. This is often called a *devolution,* instead of evolution, a proceeding downward instead of proceeding upward. Of course, at this stage, very few people pass downward in this way; there is only an occasional case.

In our study of after-death states you may remember that H. P. B. divided the astral and the mental into kamic, kama-manasic, and lower manasic: that was one of her divisions. You have here a triple division—pure kama (mere animal passion); kama-manasic (mentality mixed with these, thus producing the emotional life); and then the lower manasic, the mind, purified from the disruptive influences of passion and emotion, and becoming a relatively pure mentality, with the personal emotions, which were pure and unselfish in their character, added to the mind as an enrichment.

Now kama, or desire, or the animal instincts, may, in the ordinary civilized human body, be said to die with the body; that is, the mind has so controlled the purely animal instincts and has so transmuted them into emotions, that it has drawn all the higher life out of them, and when the physical body dies and the etheric double disintegrates, there is only a practically lifeless shell left of the purely animal instincts. That is just round the man as he passes into purgatory, or kamaloka, but it is not vivified enough, nor enough in touch with him, for him to be conscious of it. He has drawn out of it all that was human in the desire-life and has lifted that on to the upper part of the astral, into the emotional world—the kama-manasic. Hence it is a mere shell, a concentric shell, around him; but nothing comes through that to him from those lower sub-planes in the astral. They cannot effect him. That sphere is filled largely with criminals, with murderers, with profligates, with suicides, and so on. These cannot communicate with the ego in this astral body; he has won away from all that during his physical life. There is practically nothing in him that responds to that; he has drawn out of it all the life that is his.

On that we may just pause for a moment that you may realize that those animal instincts are hardly recognized in your thought for exactly what they are. In the animal, they are an essential part of his life, and dominate his consciousness, his existence. He is driven by them. The brute is moved by these, and they are stimulated from the astral and physical planes. The man in the savage state is still largely under these, and, as long as he is under them, he is, from the occult standpoint, a savage. He is not really a man, he is an animal-man; and the stages remaining in him of the animal life are not eliminated life after life, but their forces must be gradually drawn into him. These lower forces are forces, and are therefore valuable; but if they dominate, they are destructive of the human. If they are controlled and drawn upward into the emotional sphere, then they make a very powerful emotional nature, which is very valuable to the man, because out of that his motive power is to be made.

Naturally in the struggle between the purely animal instincts and the higher emotions built into them, in the midst of the struggle against the domination of the lower, many tendencies remain that we regard as being evil, because they hold us back, and you must obtain a repulsive force sufficient to transmute these. What is wanted is not that these forces shall be killed out, but that they shall be transmuted. The force is really valuable, but it is destructive if allowed to play about in the lower matter of the astral plane. That is always what is meant by purification—the transmutation of those forces into higher expressions of life.

Of course, up to a very considerable stage of civilization, these play by far too great a part in the life of the average man. But if you will study the scheme of evolution as laid down by the Manu, you will see how carefully that scheme is planned to utilize and lift them, so that when the man has lived through his life he has practically eliminated that side before he passes through the gateway of death. The whole of the castes, most markedly in the Brahmana and the Kshattriya, are especially arranged for this purpose, and in those castes exists the most perfect scheme of human evolution that has ever been devised. The fact that you see around you now a mere tangled remnant of the system ought not to blind you to the fundamental value of the whole conception of what was necessary for the co-operation of the human with the deva worlds, the man recognizing his duty, and the deva guiding the man back to the exact stage in the physical world where he would find the duty which was fit for him at the stage of evolution he had reached.

Now that, in its perfection, existed only in the Root-stock of the Aryan Race. Of course it exists through the whole race as a principle in the types and temperaments, but there was not elsewhere the same correlation between the human and the guiding worlds. That correlation is now practically broken by the failure of the human to co-operate, and now there is the confusion and the turmoil which you all know; hence, only very rarely now is there the guidance of a soul that has reached a particular stage into the body suitable for that stage, and therefrom comes the confusion, and comes also the necessity to re-cast the whole thing because it is no longer real. It has become a mere sham at the present time.

When that was perfectly worked out, as it was in its early stages, you had the whole of this transmutation process going on, life after life, until the man became fit for Initiation, and passed onward through the stages of Initiation into Liberation, or Salvation.

The clear understanding of that is useful, but it should be generally realized that if a man wants to escape from any consciousness after death on these lower sub-planes, he must have totally eliminated from himself the purely passional (kamic), and during his physical life he must have transmuted passions into emotions. There must no longer be passions, because if they still exist on leaving the body, the man must be conscious on the whole of the lower sub-planes, and that means a miserable existence for a time. You know what it would be for any of you now to be confined to the society of criminals, murderers, suicides, and so on, and what a horrible thing you would feel that to be. Yet it is the inevitable result of the existence of what we call the animal desire-nature at the time of death. It is far harder to fight through after death than it is here, even though the struggle may be great on this side. If it is left, any of it, to the other side of death, you are forced into the struggle; you can't help it then. Then it is a matter of pure patience, a starving out of an agonizing instinct. And there lies the absolute folly of a human being who allows that to remain master during his physical life, when he is the best able to dominate it, for it is enormously more difficult to dominate it on the other side.

In the study of some of our early literature, students find a difficulty, because its nomenclature is different from that which we use today, but they should familiarize themselves with the old as well as the new. It is really helpful, and it is very good for you to have your categories broken up occasionally, so that they shall not hold you and make you rigid and unreceptive. There is always the danger of the student, when he begins his study, forgetting that a classification is made for use and ought not to tie him down. It is only to help you to understand certain things more definitely and more clearly. If instead of using it you let it dominate you, then it becomes a hindrance.

You want to learn things, let us say. Then you rearrange them as you want them for a particular kind of study, as is done in every science. If you are studying psycho-physiology, you get the division of body and mind, and the reactions of one upon the other. In order to study these, you want those two divisions only, to see how they react upon each other. But suppose you wish to study the physical body, its physiology. Then you at once begin to subdivide that in other ways. You may subdivide it into organs, according to functions—heart, brain, lungs, stomach, and all the rest, and those are perfectly true subdivisions. But you have divided them in that way because you want to understand the functions of the body, and therefore you take the organs as a subject for study. But suppose, instead of that, you wanted to understand the minute anatomy of the body. Then you would not trouble about these organs. You would think simply of the materials of the body, and you would divide it up into bone, muscular tissue, connective tissue, nerve tissue, and so on. There is no real confusion in that. Each division clarifies your study.

I notice, however, in our Theosophical studies, that very often those of our members who have gone through a scientific training get very confused and muddled over our different categories. "Oh, this contradicts that," they say. It is just as though, when you are dealing with muscular tissue, you should say that it is in the heart, and later on when you were dealing with connective tissue, you should say that it is in the heart also. Then the student might say: "I was told that there was muscular tissue in the heart; now you are telling me that there is connective tissue. Which is true?"

As you gain exact knowledge, your knowledge divides itself according to its nature, and as you study the occult view of the world, as you study your own constitution from the occult standpoint, you want different divisions from time to time according to the object of your study. You remember how I have pointed out to you that in studying Yoga you deal with a duality—spirit and matter. That is all you want. You want to realize in your study of Yoga that there is a duality. There is the spirit-side; there is the form-side. And so you get the two fundamental divisions that you need in Yoga, where all the bodies are treated as one body, where all the phases of consciousness are treated as one consciousness; for you want in Yoga to realize consciousness and vehicles. You do not want for the moment to divide the matter up into all its phases. Your first duty is to separate man into a duality. That does not alter the fact that he is also a septenary, a quaternary, and a triad. Exactly according to the points of your study you should divide things, and you will never get confused if you study facts. Get all the descriptions, all the subdivisions and the divisions you can, and then get hold of the facts under each. When you thoroughly understand the facts, you can divide them up according to the particular thing that you want to study.

In one of our earlier classifications we had the lower triad and the higher quaternary—physical, astral, mental, and Intellect, Buddhi, Atma, Monad. That was a division between the mortal and the immortal, and that was an excellent way for the study of that difference. There comes eventually the struggle between those two, the mortal and the immortal. The mortal part, kama-manas and the lower manas (desire-mind and lower mind)—that has to die. It struggles for its life. The immortal part must either draw out of that all that is valuable, and so enrich itself with the product of the life-period that is over, carrying the whole of that into the immortal part in order to build up the next personality, or it must lose it. And that is the struggle that takes place between the upper astral and the devachanic life. The struggle is practically over when the man takes into the mental body the most valuable part of the emotions. While he is living in the higher astral world his work is to draw the purely unselfish part away from the astral body, to bring that into the mental body and carry it on into Devachan.

Then comes the second stage of unconsciousness, and to describe this the word second death has always been used, but it is in a very subordinate sense. It is preceded by a period of varying length, because the length depends upon the quantity of emotions, the good but rather selfish emotions, that are to be worked out in the stage which is sometimes called the "summerland." The part of a man's love for the God whom he worships, which has been connected always with thoughts of reward, that is worked out in that part of the lower heaven that he has thought about down here—the Jerusalem of the Christian, the streets of gold, the palms, and so on, the pitri-loka of the Hindu. It is the region where one works out the good emotions which were strongly tinged with desire for personal gain, the devotion to God which is not unselfish, but looks for some return which it wishes to enjoy; it is not giving, but taking.

There is no harm in that; it is not to be regarded in any sense as wrong. It is a necessary stage, but it is mortal, and it belongs to the higher astral world. And so with all those forms of intellectual and scientific work which are connected with the physical brain processes with all the apparatus of science, the methods of science for working out experiments, and so on. You will find people like Darwin, Clifford, and others in that higher region of the astral world, and they remain there for a long time. All philanthropic work in which the lower has mingled to a considerable extent keeps the person there.

All this goes on till the selfish element is eliminated. When that is eliminated, the man falls asleep, as it were, and the pure mind, the concrete mind, wakes up in Devachan, and there, as you know, the life consists in working up all the materials of emotion and mentality into a lasting form, the germ of faculty, to be communicated to the higher mind in the causal body.

Thus you have your phases of post-mortem existence. All the unselfish personal emotions are worked up into capacity for emotion. Hence you will see why what is called a "strong personality" is of very great value. You want all the force out of it, with all the selfishness eliminated; but you do not want to lose the force; you want to transmute it to the service of the higher. The stages where the personality is weak, in the ordinary sense of the term—not dominated, but weak—those are the lower stages of the continually repeated evolution. The man is born over and over and over again, in order that he may accumulate force, because without an enormous accumulation of force there is not enough of him to go on. This repeated rebirth does not mean that he is blameworthy but that he has not grown up. He is in the child-stage, the stage where his desires will gradually teach him. He is not ready for anything higher, for he must grow. That growth, of course, can be very much quickened when a person has reached a fair stage of understanding, and here comes in the advantage of Theosophical knowledge. The ordinary human being is working in the dark. He has passions, emotions, and he does not know exactly what to do with them. He knows vaguely that he must master his passions, that he must not run after some one else's wife; that he understands and he dominates it. He does not realize the value of the feeling that he dominates, the force in it, and he does not know how to transmute it. He rather tries to kill it.

The great lesson of Occultism is: "Do not kill, but transmute." Realize that every force of nature is to be regarded simply as a force. Evolution consists in mastering those forces. There is the force of electricity, but it is not moral or immoral; it is without morality. It is simply a force. You utilize it by the apparatus by which you guide it along a particular line. You may guide it along a line where it is useful, as in wire telegraphy. You may guide it along a line where it is destructive, as in using it for explosions. Yet it is the same force. You do not, if you want to do much useful work, weaken your cells, but you prepare an apparatus to guide the current to the work you require performed. So you do not weaken the force which is rushing along undesirable channels, but you send it along channels which turn it to a noble purpose, and thus perform great work.

The whole task of human evolution is to learn how to use these forces, and the crime of modern science is that it has learned about many forces and seen how to control them, and is turning them to frightfully destructive purposes, such as have made this War an unexampled horror. There is science turned to the lower purposes. You cannot blame Nature. Every force that western science is using to destroy is a force which ought to have been turned to the helping of life, to its preservation, to the happiness of man. So you can see very plainly, by what is going on in Europe now, how wise the Master K. H. was when he said, as published in *The Occult World,* that They would not help science until the social conscience was developed. We have seen what science is without conscience. There is no growth of the social conscience in the western world with regard to the use of science. Every great scientific man in the Nations is using all his brain-power, his knowledge, his authority over Nature, to turn her forces to the service of the powers of destruction—the dark powers, the dark brotherhood.

What we have to realize is that the western world, for want of the social conscience, of the sentiment of duty to man as man, has turned science to the most devilish purposes for which it could be used, and is thereby creating a terrible karma. One cannot judge, one has no right to judge, how this thing has gone on from one stage to another. The beginning of it was the gross materialism of science in the latter part of the nineteenth century; and there again, if you trace it backward to discover why science was so materialistic, you will find it was because religion had so persecuted it. You see how all these things are interlinked. If for a moment you could imagine that there had been no Middle Ages with the Roman Catholic Church in power, destroying the scientists of the time, burning, torturing, imprisoning the scientific thinkers of the day, you would have a better idea of one of the phases of the karma of the present time. Then you have to go back to the ignorance of which the result was to set religion against science. Thus the evil karma was made. Science turned against religion for its life's sake. You cannot blame the scientific men; they were fighting for their life, and everything they could discover which showed religion that it was wrong was a gain. I never blame them, because I see the difficulty they were in; if they were to progress in science they had to cripple religion, which had become a mere persecuting agency. Actually, they did it. Thus they conquered a free platform, but with it materialism. Materialism was denser in Germany than elsewhere; hence Germany took the lead in this particular phase of misapplication of science and became the tool of the dark powers. But, looking at the whole thing, personally I could not particularly blame Germany for that. One sees how it grew stage by stage; ignorance, Catholicism, Lutheranism, persecution, scientific struggle, conflict with religion, triumph of free thought. So you come to the tremendous springing forward of science, and the negation of all human brotherhood and human relationship, and the utilizing of science for two main purposes—the getting of money, and the finding out of ways to destroy.

How are they going to escape from this karmic tangle? I can't say. It seems to me just one of the stages where some greater Being is necessary for the salvation of the world; and so the great Teacher is coming. No power less than His can lift the world out of the stage into which it has fallen. And that is why I have recently laid so much stress on our urgent duty to give to the Hierarchy the co-operation for which that Hierarchy is asking, it being the first time in the history of evolution that They can attain their object without destroying the whole civilization, as They did in Atlantis, and on a smaller scale in Rome.

Therefore I ask you at the present time not to think so much of your own personal progress, but rather to throw all your force into the helping of the world. Try to do your share of this great work, and try to get rid of those elements in yourselves which are on the wrong side. We have plenty of lives more to learn in; at the present time we have not time to learn, except the lessons that come by experience, which, after all, are a good deal more useful than those that come by teaching.

CHAPTER III

THE YUCATAN BROTHERHOOD

Many of you may, perhaps, know that the impulse which originated the Spiritualistic movement came from the White Lodge itself, and was passed through certain Initiates and Disciples of the Fourth Race; and it is that which gave it its peculiar character. Most of you have doubtless heard of the Brotherhood of Yucatan, in Mexico, an exceedingly remarkable group of Occultists, who came down by definite succession in Fourth Race bodies, maintaining the Fourth Race methods of occult progress.

They play quite a definite part in connection with the Fourth Race, which, as you know, includes the great majority of the people now in the world. That is sometimes forgotten. We are apt to think of the Fifth Race, with which we are all immediately connected, as the main Race in the World; whereas, as a matter of fact, the Fourth Race is enormously greater in numbers.

The Fifth Race, which is leading evolution, is a minority. In fact, that is the normal rule of progress, that a minority leads, and then gradually the others come up to its level, while it itself passes onward. So, out of the Fifth Race the most advanced will pass on to the Sixth Root Race; and then the

Fifth Race will gradually become a majority, and the Fourth Race, like the Third now, will become the laggard minority behind the bulk.

Hence this Brotherhood of Yucatan plays an important part in the evolution of the world in connection with the Fourth Race. Its methods are more suitable to that Race. They are not the later methods of Those whom we speak of as the great White Lodge, chosen for the Fifth Race evolution. This does not mean that in that Lodge itself there are not Those who have come up from the Fourth Race. They all have come from it. But it means that They are utilizing bodies whose nervous constitution is very much finer, is more highly organized, especially those who in the decadence of the Fourth Race went on under the special guidance of the White Lodge of the time, and took up methods which were specially intended to save the Fifth Race from the catastrophe in which a majority of the Fourth Race were overwhelmed in the great cataclysm of Atlantis. None the less, as I say, the Fourth Race remains the majority, and this Occult Brotherhood of Yucatan is specially charged with looking after them. Their methods have always been —as were Fourth Race methods of the past—those which dealt with the advance of mankind through what is called now "the lower psychism"; that is, through a number of occult phenomena connected with the physical plane and tangible, so that, on the physical plane, proofs might be afforded of the reality of the hidden worlds. That was the object of it, as it has always been.

It was found that the results of that method tended, after a time, rather to materialize religion. People sought for phenomena rather than for spirituality, and sought to prove the spiritual by the material. The methods were therefore left only to those who preferred them and to whom they were most suitable, while the Fifth Race was trained along a more difficult, but surer path, in which knowledge had to be gained side by side with the evolution, not of the emotional and passional, but of the mental, nature. They had to pass through the intellect to the higher intuition, or as it is sometimes called, "the higher psychism."

Hence, when it was seen that the Fifth Race was drifting into materialism in its most advanced members, the scientific world, and that knowledge was progressing much faster than the social conscience and moral evolution, it was thought necessary to start a movement which would appeal to those who were materialistically-minded, and would afford them a certain amount of proof, tangible on the physical plane, of the reality of the superphysical, of the unseen, though not of the spiritual, worlds.

Hence the Spiritualist Movement. That proceeded in the western world by demonstrations available to physical investigation, by knocking, by tilting of material objects, such as tables, chairs, or anything else that was conveniently movable. Later on, there were voices that were made audible, and still later what is called "materialization"; that is, persons clothed in the astral body, who had laid aside their physical bodies either temporarily or permanently, took from people who were constituted in a particular way, parts of the etheric double and even parts of the dense physical body, so that their astral bodies, thickened, densified, by this material addition, might become visible to ordinary sight. With all its disadvantages, it was the only method available, and therefore of course was taken to prevent the catastrophe of the universal spread of materialistic science over the Nations, which were at that time influencing the intellectual life of the world.

The Yucatan Brotherhood, accustomed to the use of that method, handed down from ancient days, took up the guidance of this rescue movement. Sometimes, in the early days of the Theosophical Society, its Masters Themselves manifested in this fashion; at other times, They spoke and taught through H. P. Blavatsky, who had a very strongly mediumistic body, due to the intermixture of Fourth Race blood (the Tartar blood in the Russian body that she took for that purpose); during the training she underwent at the hands of a Master of the White Lodge, by which she reached a very high degree of knowledge and power, she learned how to utilize her body and to keep it under her own control, permitting it to be used by others only with her own consent.

It was this peculiar mixture of mediumistic body and occult development which made H. P. B. so very puzzling a person to those among whom she lived. There was the Fourth Race strain, highly developed, which made her, as the Master said, the most wonderfully developed psychic that had been born for two hundred years; and there was the careful training of all the higher powers, which jointly made it possible for Them to utilize her as a physical medium for Themselves.

Now the need for careful training of the sensitive lies in the fact that if such a person is left to himself or herself, they, being without knowledge, are not able to protect themselves, and to select those whom they will permit to use their physical bodies. In the earlier days, they were protected by priests in the Temples, and were the sibyls and vestal virgins of the older religions. They were scrupulously guarded from contact with the other world, and only chosen persons were allowed to come near them. But when such people, in a time of ignorance of Occultism, came into the world, and were exposed to all its difficulties without any kind of outer protection, they became the ordinary mediums of the last century, who could not protect themselves at all. They were open to every influence which came from the astral world and from the higher regions of the physical world. Hence they were mostly in touch with the less developed human beings who had passed on, the crowds of average people who throng the lower reaches of the astral world. While some of the Yucatan Brothers guarded very carefully their own special disciples, that they might give higher teachings through them, there were many mediums who were left practically uncared for, save when some kindly discarnate entity, attracted by some good quality in them, guarded them to some extent, warding off influences from the evil-minded of the astral world.

Materialization is not so marked now as it was in the earlier days, when we find that very many of the "controls" were North American Indians. It was very characteristic of the early phases. It began in America, of course, where the available people were, so to speak, most handy, and you find a number of American Indians acting as controls of those first mediums. They were given all sorts of names, such as "Sunshine," and the like. When they materialized, they materialized in their own forms, which very often were those of children.

Then came a phase where others, not Indians, but people of somewhat the same type, materialized, showing through their communications that they were ignorant and undeveloped. But these crude messages were sometimes interspersed with communications of great value, coming from some member of this Occult Brotherhood, or even, on a few occasions, directly from the White Lodge. In the case of Stainton Moses you are face to face with such an illustration; a man of high intellectual value, full of doubts, full of questionings, and therefore not very suitable for an average medium, who needs to be quite passive. Because of his intellectuality a very high use was made of him, and some of the teachings which came through him were of great value. Through some of the American mediums also some fine teachings came, and you have this mingled mass of messages of very varying usefulness.

The real value of Spiritualism was that it gave tangible proofs of post-mortem existence, so that a man like Sir William Crookes was able in his laboratory, by applying the most careful scientific methods of investigation, to obtain quite definite proofs of existences other than the physical. You can read his own records, and see the remarkable scientific acumen that he brought to bear on his investigations; see how he invented a particular kind of light, so that the materialized bodies should not be broken up, as they were by ordinary light; how he invented a method of weighing the materialized form, and so on. Those methods are still followed by the Italian and French investigators, who were all of the type of materialistic scientists, and who one after another emerged from materialism into Spiritualism. They do not always call themselves Spiritualists, shrinking from the name, but they have published their investigations most fully; they are men like Rochas and Richet in France, both largely tinged with Theosophy, and Lombroso, in Italy, who obtained a most remarkable series of proofs.

The scientists were sufficient to give to the scientific world, if it chose to look into their records, the proofs which it demanded; as a rule, scientists would not look into them.. The Royal Society still refuses to recognize Crookes's fine investigations. He very nearly lost his position as a Fellow of the Royal Society, because he was regarded as superstitious and as going into illegitimate speculations. However, he recorded his proofs, and he endorses down to the present day the validity of his own investigations. Sir Oliver Lodge has, to some extent, followed in his steps.

So far as Spiritualism went along the line on which it was intended to go, it was exceedingly useful at that time, and remains useful now. It is the one line of physical proof of superphysical facts, apart from all questions either of moral worth or of spiritual unfolding. Anybody can, as in ordinary physical science, obtain proofs who chooses to follow the methods, and a good many scientists have followed them. Sir Oliver Lodge, as said, is one of them; he has published a remarkable book, called *Raymond*, in which the evidence of post-mortem existence is taken from his son, who was killed on one of the battlefields of the present War.

Now, of course, the present time offers innumerable facilities in that way. Hosts of young men are flung out of mortal life in the full vigor of their manhood and cannot quickly pass on into the Devachanic existence. They are suddenly killed, and that brings about, as you know, peculiar karma. Moreover, the conditions in the astral world just now are much changed. People are no longer under the ordinary rules, which were far better for them—unless they have reached a very considerable height of unfolding—practically to fall asleep, to gather up all the experiences of the life that are useful, to carry them on to Devachan, and work them out into faculty. Instead of that the whole thing is now changed. People who die normally, not by accident, are continually being retained there for special work, and very large numbers, nearly all of you perhaps, will not pass out of this life into the devachanic existence; most of you will probably choose to come back (if you pass away within a few years), in order to be with the Lord Maitreya when He comes, or to work at the enormous volume of work which will have to be done when He has left the world again, at the stage which He Himself has brought about, but which will need reinforcing and further evolution.

CHAPTER IV

THE UNCONSCIOUSNESS PRECEDING DEVACHAN

The Monad, in the sense in which we use that term today, is that divine emanation which exists on the sixth plane and upward. To all intents and purposes he is unconscious in the lower world. His consciousness on his own plane is complete; he shares the divine knowledge in his own world, but he cannot reach down any further. He cannot in any way touch the lower planes of life, the matter there being of a character which is not amenable to his influences. He, who has been in union with all around him, if plunged into denser matter, would find himself in uttermost isolation, as in empty space, unconscious of all impacts and contacts of matter. Hence the whole of his evolutionary journey, down and again upward, is for the purpose of acquiring that consciousness, of subjugating matter completely as a vehicle, until on each plane he answers to the vibrations of similar matter outside, and is able to bring out moods of consciousness, which answer to those outside impressions, and thereby to become conscious of them.

In one of our previous talks you will remember that I laid stress upon the fact that you only know impressions, the results on your own consciousness of something that happens outside. Gradually by these impressions you gain knowledge of the outside world. Of course it is really knowledge of the impressions made upon you by the outside world; the knowledge of the outside world in reality is only gained when you reach the stage of evolution in which, having realized the unity of life, you are able to live in all those forms below; only then does real knowledge of the outside world come to you at all.

As long as you are separate in your consciousness, you can only receive impressions made upon you, and those impressions form to you your outside world. But when you have realized the One Life, when you are able to pass into any form at will, then you become able really to know the outside world, because you live in the forms which make up that world, and you are no longer dealing with the impressions they make upon your consciousness, but with their consciousness, as you exist within their own forms—a very, very different thing.

That is the fundamental reason why this world is called "unreal." You do not know it as it is; you are not in a world of reality; you are living in a world of your own creation, made partly by these impressions from outside. An enormous change of attitude comes when, instead of knowing the impression a thing makes upon us, we live within the thing, and know that thing from inside by virtue of the One Life which we have realized. That enormous change means an entire revolution in our ideas. But it can come to us only when the Life is realized. Then everything becomes in a sense real to us, because we are the Life in a special form at the time, and we can correlate all those together, and then understand.

In the Monad we have a fragment of the One Life. Everything is in that, by virtue of the One Life that he shares, but it has to be brought out. That is why we sometimes speak of "awakening into life the latent consciousness." Literally everything is in that Monad, all divine knowledge; but to bring that out, so that on any plane of matter he may *know*, is the whole work of evolution. That is the mysterious pressure which puzzles science so much, as to why things move onward; what is the force which makes for evolution? Why is it that the various lives, as they call them, moving in different directions, yet are related one to the other? What gives rise to all this variety?

The answer is that this "latent consciousness has to be awakened into life"; that is, awakened to Self-consciousness. And in order that this memory of all the things and the persons that you have vivified in the past may awaken within you, the Monad has joined himself to the highest attributes of the lower personality.

I ought, perhaps, to tell you that there is a very considerable difference between this awakening of what was in the old days called the "personal individuality," and what is normally called the "memory of past lives." It is perfectly possible to gain a knowledge of your past lives from observation from without, that is to say, by clairvoyance which, looking back through the ages, recognizes your own activity in any particular life, and watches that as you might watch the life of anybody else. That is what is generally called "the memory of past lives." It is not really a memory; it is an observation from outside;

you see yourself living and moving, and in that way you get a good record of the life.

The memory of past lives which is to be awakened in the Monad is a very much more intimate thing. It is the inner recognition, not the outer observation alone, of the life, and that is really the only thing to which the word "memory" ought accurately to be applied. You may remember Mr. Leadbeater telling us one day how he found dates in the past: he found the date by looking into the mind of somebody, and seeing what persons were thought of as contemporaries by that man; or, if that person happened to have it, the date of that particular year in which he was living. Mr. Leadbeater was not that person, but he was able so to look at the consciousness of the person as to be able to get information out of it. If you think of that as an observation of another, you will realize exactly what I mean when I say that you may know your past lives by observation. You may observe yourself just as you might observe anybody else. You can look into your own mind of the past, just as you can look into the mind of anybody else; but it is all from outside.

Now there is a subtle change when, instead of observing either the person's acts in his body, or his emotions, or his thoughts, the whole of these are fully realized as one's own, and when one distinguishes between these and all the various persons around as the "I" and the "not-I." Of course the first is very much the easier, and is the more common, simply because many have got on far enough to reach that point.

When the true memory is unfolded in the Monad—which means that the Monad has assimilated what he has put forth—then (to use the old phraseology) the three aspects of the higher, the Atma, the Buddhi, and the Manas, which we used to call the triad, have been drawn back into the Monad, and his content has been increased by all that; then he must also acquire the highest attributes of the desire-mind (kama-manasic) being, which is the conscious person in each life, that in which we are living all the time. That is really the personal ego, that which to all ordinary people is the waking consciousness of the "I."

It is that which, purified, lives and enjoys bliss in Devachan, this kama-manasic entity, purified from the lower kinds of kama. It is that which lives in Devachan.

It is important to remember that the "I" cannot "assimilate anything that is evil," because it enables you to realize that certain actions that we call evil, done by the undeveloped person, have not the same results as they have when done by the more highly developed person. They do not touch the "I" level of thought. The ego is not conscious of them; he knows nothing about them, and so they make no impression on him. The utmost—I think it was printed in one of our publications—the utmost result that is brought about in the causal body by very, very long continued lives of a low type is what you may call a certain incapacity to receive the opposite good impression for a very considerable period afterwards, a kind of numbness or paralysis of the matter there; not consciousness at all, but an unconsciousness, and an unconsciousness which resists impressions of the good of the opposite kind. That is the limit of the harm that is done. It makes many more lives necessary in order to bring out the first response to the good side of activity. That is what happens to the causal body, where the animal-man life has been very much prolonged.

We have not looked into the causes as to why it should be so; it was only the result which we noticed one time when we were trying to understand how the causal body was living through all these earlier savage lives, and how it was that it was not apparently injured. We found that in very prolonged cases, where there was an abnormal number of such lives, there was a certain effect of numbness. It could not respond, but the repeated beating of evil upon it produced this curious effect of numbness, or partial paralysis, which had gradually to be worn off, so that a number of lives had to be spent in, as it were, restoring the responsive vitality to that portion of the causal body. Those are abnormal cases.

In some of our earliest teachings a great deal of stress was laid upon the unconscious condition into which men sink between the highest sub-plane of Kama-loka and the lowest sub-plane of Devachan, that which H. P. B. spoke of as a "laya-centre," the transition state between the two, which was neither one nor the other, and in which we were told that the man stays very long, sometimes longer than we can imagine. The stay in Kama-loka you cannot fix at any particular period. In the less evolved stage the stay there is involuntary, the working out, of course, of the results of the evil or the passion side of the nature. In the higher sub-planes of Kama-loka the stay is voluntary, and depends on the will of the man himself.

You know we have said to you that the scientific people, who have clung very much to their scientific methods, remain on these high sub-planes of Kamaloka for a very long time. They remain just as long as they choose to remain, as long as they like that way of working. The very idea of giving up their methods is to them so repellent that they prefer to remain in that condition. I think I told you once of a great scientist who will not go out of it; he wants to work in the way that he worked as a scientist here, and somehow he does not realize that he can work very much better, if he himself uses his own faculties in their own world than he can with his astral apparatus. He wants the apparatus that he can construct over there, and finds it so very wonderful that he likes to use it, and the fact that he was skeptical here, the fact that he did not think that personal consciousness went on at all after death, that very fact remains with him, and makes him doubt a life beyond his present condition, in the same way that Charles Bradlaugh does. He told me one day: "Yes, you were right in saying I should go on after death, but I can't tell that I shall go on further if I again become unconscious." It is that period of unconsciousness that alarms them; they are going, so to speak, to die again. Finding this life so very full of knowledge and so superior to the one here, extending their knowledge of the universe continuously in this way, they cannot realize that it is better to throw the whole of that apparatus away, to trust for a time to the word of people who have gone through these conditions many times before, to trust to them that the greater freedom of the inner faculties will more than compensate for the absence of the outer apparatus—they cannot do this. Therefore they remain there; they will not enter the "period of gestation."

The same is the case with one of those persons who is always living in a library; he gets the astral counterpart of all the books that are written now, and he enjoys himself enormously; and there is no apparent reason why he should not stay there for the rest of the cycle; he won't get out. So you cannot fix any time for this period.

But as to this period of unconsciousness, it is a condition that in these later times we have not gone into and studied, and I think we ought to study it, because really it remains to us very much of a name. It is evidently a period quite necessary to the building up of the devachanic ego for the life in Devachan, and that apparently may be a very long period. Just as in the womb of the mother the body of the child is built up, so in this gestation period what you may call the body for Devachan is built up. One thing that must take place in it is the separating off of all the astral matter, however subtle that astral matter may be; that must be left behind. The man practically goes to sleep and is unconscious. During that period of unconsciousness, all that is useful which has been worked into the astral matter, that is, all the higher emotions, the astral matter connected with the whole of those modes of consciousness, is separated off from the matter through which they were expressed, or which brought them out, and the vibrations of the matter connected with those, which have been spread over the whole of the astral body of this particular phase of matter, the whole of those are directed on to the permanent atom, and the permanent atom responds, taking up the power of vibrating in these measures, and thus preserves everything for the next astral body. And all that is valuable for the higher life—the feeling of devotion, the feeling of unselfish love, either for a person or for a cause, everything in your emotional life which is of a higher kind—and the whole of that must have a material basis, you must remember—the whole of that is transferred as a vibratory power to the permanent astral atom, and that in turn produces sympathetic vibrations in the mental atom, from which every one of those vibrations of the higher kind, which had been expressed in the finer matter of the astral body, is sent through the mental body, and affects the moods of the mental consciousness.

Now it is quite intelligible that that might occupy a considerable period of time, and that the more of it there is, the longer the time which will be required. It is really the drawing out of the life on which certain impressions have been made, or the centering of them in the permanent atom, which, you must always remember, only preserves the capacity of vibration. Do not think of the permanent atom as some kind of box into which you can pack more and more emotion or thought forms; that is not at all the way to look upon it. It does not preserve vibrations, but it has the capacity to reproduce vibrations, and that capacity can only be aroused by having vibrated before in that particular way. That, as you can imagine, might take a considerable time, especially as it is to a certain extent a mechanical process.

Another considerable part of that unconscious, or gestation, period must be spent in vivifying for separate life the mental matter which had always been vivified during the earth-life and the post-mortem life on the astral plane through the kamic elements. You see the whole of our physical life is kama-manasic work; the whole of our emotional and mental life is also kama-manasic work, and that forms the personal ego and the personal existence. In the physical life, while we are awake, the mental life is working, of course, in connection with the physical body; but while we are asleep it is working in the astral body. After we pass through death the physical body is gone, but the mental is continuing the life it is accustomed to in the sleep-life, active on the astral plane; and as soon as it is on the astral plane it must have astral matter to work there. Hence I imagine the need of that gestation period, which we have overlooked so much, is also to vivify the mental body for a separated existence, when it has lost its lifelong partner. When this kamic element is got rid of altogether, the ego in the region of bliss, or Devachan, will have the purified memory. It will not remember anything that has been unpleasant; it will not remember anything that has been wrong or evil or degrading in any way, anything that is mingled with the lower passions. The whole of that is gone; hence the unalloyed bliss.

That enables you to understand from the mechanical standpoint what is called the artificial guardianship of Devachan. Do not think of that as a kind of artificial wall built around a certain space, but realize that a gulf exists round each individual there, because of the fact that the whole of the kamic matter has been swept away and is no longer there. He has no vehicle, no medium of communication, which can respond to anything of the lower worlds. Therefore the lower worlds for him are non-existent, but non-existent for exactly the same reason that the higher worlds are to a number of us non-existent. We have not vitalized to a proper extent the matter through which we can communicate with the matter of those worlds. You have not round you an outside wall excluding you, but it is in you yourself; and the process of getting into touch with the higher worlds is in breaking through this inner wall round you and in yourself; or, in other words, you have vitalized the matter of the mental body for direct communication with your lower sheaths; it is already there, present in you, but it is not working on its own account, and is not at once able to cross this "laya-centre" between the planes.

Before going on to the awakening into Devachan, let us consider for a moment the people whom H. P. B. spoke of as "soul-less," those who have overstepped the boundary of human evolution through persistent "wickedness," and who are devoluting, as it is sometimes called. They are going backward instead of evolving, having broken away from the mental and spiritual essence of their being.

Some of these resume their evolution, taking new lower bodies, and are merely thrown back in evolution; others, of the lower type (who after their physical and during their astral life have lost their lower permanent atoms) will have to retire until the stage of a new world opens, suitable for the very low level of evolution at which they left this world by death. They pass into what is called the "planetary death," and when they come back into a new world, will take fresh lower permanent atoms from its matter.

Meanwhile the astral body, with the astral and

physical permanent atoms, and the mental body interwoven with the astral, torn away from the Spirit, is too strongly vivified to disintegrate, and incarnates again in a body of a very low type; when this physical body dies, a yet lower human incarnation follows, perhaps as an idiot, then devolves into an animal, and sinks downward lower and lower, to final disintegration into the elements.

In the normal man, to whom we now return, when the mental matter is vivified sufficiently to work independently, the next stage follows, the awakening on the rupa levels of Devachan. The man is shut off from the lower worlds by the purifying of the mental body from all foreign elements, and it is important to realize that this absence of the astral is the gulf that separates him from the lower worlds. He is shut into the world made by his own impressions of those worlds, a separating wall of exactly the same nature as that which separates us down here, where each lives in his own mental world; but he can communicate with other persons through mental bodies, as down here through physical ones. That is why sometimes in the older writings each one is spoken of as being shut off. He is shut off from these lower worlds and shut in within his own mental world. The karma of the recollection of evil deeds and feelings will reach the ego when it changes its personality in the following world of causes; that is, in its next birth into mortal life. The spiritual individuality remains untouched in all cases while it is in the higher world.

The period spent in Devachan is according to the good karma that a man takes with him. He has to turn all good experience into faculty. If he takes little, it is short; if he takes an average amount, it is an average length; if he takes an exceptional amount, an exceptional length. It is impossible to lay down any definite duration at all. He reaps faculty where he sowed experience, and when the whole of that is assimilated, the thirst for physical life revives. That is what brings the man back; he wants to come; he is hungry, in fact, for more of the lower things and senses and vibrations, and he becomes hungry the moment he has completely assimilated everything which in the past life he gathered. It is worth while to remember that, because it is a question often asked you, and rather confused answers are sometimes given. It is not an outside pressure that drives him back, but he comes because he wants to come. It is all nonsense about people wanting to come back or not; they would not come back if they did not want to, but as long as any desire remains for anything this world can give them, they want to come back; it is because *they* want to come that they come, not because somebody else wants them to come. It is not the pressure of any superior power which drives them, against their will, back to this world of troubles, but the intense hunger for it.

It corresponds to your own condition in the physical body when you have taken food and it has all been assimilated. You want more. You go and get food; no one has to drive you to it; you get it because you want it. As long as man is imperfect, as long as he has not assimilated everything this world can give, and utilized it to the full, so that he does not want anything more here, so long will he return.

There is a lower kind of Moksha that it is quite

possible to get. A great many people in this country get it by a deliberate killing out of all desire for objects of enjoyment. They remain away for indefinite periods of time, and remain in what is practically arupa Devachan. The disadvantage of it is that you only put off the day of Liberation; you may put it off to another world—remember that is quite possible. A man must be born in the world to which his desires lead him. Remember what is said in the Upanishats, a man is reborn into the world to which his desires take him. As the desire of some here in India, who have given themselves very largely to meditation, is entirely toward the objects of meditation, they stay in the mental world, and that is, of course, a form of liberation. That is, they have got out of the troubles of this world, but they will only come back ultimately into the troubles of another world; and that is why it is not really worth while to do it. You may as well get your troubles over, and then have the life before you of helping the world onward. But it is impossible to put a limit to that time, because it is possible, anyhow temporarily, to kill out desire for everything here.

It is because of that power, because of that ability to "kill out," that I always say "transmute." That which you kill rises again, that which you transmute is changed for ever. The person who is in a very imperfect condition of evolution—as a great many of these good people are—if he kills out desire in that period of his evolution, he kills with it all of the possibilities of the higher evolution, because he has nothing to transmute; he has killed the thing; it is gone. It is dead for the present life, which means that all the higher life of the emotions and the mind is for the time killed; of course not altogether; it is for the time. And therefore we always try to persuade people not to follow that line. It is sometimes called the lower burning-ground; that state of mind which is brought about by an indifference which is the result of great disappointment, or trouble, or weariness of some kind, not the desire for the higher life really, but the repulsion from the lower; and the results of these are quite different.

You remember in *The Voice of Silence* it says that the soul wants points that draw upward; not the driving away of desire by failure, by disappointment, by grief, by the love becoming tasteless, because of something you have lost in it. You do not get rid of the taste for life by that; you only get rid of the taste temporarily, and it is still there and will revive.

CHAPTER V

ANSWERS TO SOME QUESTIONS

If you read the sacred books of the East you will find that it constantly happens that you come across a passage which, on the first reading, seems to be quite of the nature of fancy or legend or allegory. But if you realize the facts, as you learn them in the Theosophical teachings, you will find that the truths appear veiled to some extent in popular language; the reason for that being that a very large number of these books were written for the sake of helping those who were, generally speaking, unversed in religious knowledge.

Many of the Puranas, for instance, were specifically written in order to convey definite knowledge of science and of history to people who were not thoroughly educated, and so you have much put in the form of a story. A simple illustration of that would be where three of the early Avataras of Vishnu were represented as in the form of a fish, a tortoise, and a boar.

To the western mind, and to the eastern mind which has been trained in the western way, that sounds a little absurd at first. People in the West are accustomed to think of God as in the form of a man. That does not shock them; but to realize that God might manifest in any form below the human is to them somewhat revolting. Perhaps that feeling is not as strong now as it was before the evolutionary teachings became so widespread; but in the earlier days to take manhood into God was thought reasonable, and a kind of concession to the greatness of the human race. But to take the whole world into God, with all of its manifestations, mobile and immobile, was regarded as blasphemous to Divinity.

In India that has not been the case. "There is nothing movable nor immovable that can exist apart from Me," says Shri Krishna. It is therefore included in that belief, that everything is a part of God. Under those conditions it was a perfectly natural and intelligible thing that the great stages of evolution, as we call them, where there was a great transition from one type of life to another, should be marked by an incarnation of divine life specifically in the typical form of the epoch, or stage, or age, which was thus entered into. So you may notice that these successive Avataras of the animal type marked the distinct stages now recognized by science as the great progressive stages of the long evolution of forms upon our earth.

Hence you have, first, the fish. Of course, science recognizes perfectly that when the whole of the surface of the world was covered with water, the fish (the earliest of the vertebrate kingdom) was the first in the evolution of forms. As the waters retreated, some earth was left, but for a long time the earth was in an exceedingly muddy and slimy and marshy state; therefore you naturally come to the reptile, and so the tortoise was taken as a symbol. Later on when the solid earth formed a large part of the surface of the globe, the mammalian kingdom appeared, and that is symbolized in the form of a boar.

To the ordinary uneducated person you could not teach scientifically this truth that the kingdoms of nature succeed each other in a very definite order, but you could put this idea of the divine life taking a new step forward, in this symbolic way, which is absolutely true. And it was sufficient to remind them that, in every stage of life, God was the one upholding force.

That wider view of life, which has come to the West by science climbing up to it by observation, and then by classification and synthesis, was put in all the ancient religions as part of the religious teachings. There was then no distinction made between the knowledge of God which came through God-illumined men (so-called "revelation"), and the knowledge of God which was found by observing Nature, which is equally a form of revelation, only by a different method. Hence there was no antagonism between the two, and the whole world was enveloped in this divine atmosphere.

Therefore in reading these books, which were intended more for the populace, you must remember that much of it was put in the form that we should now call allegory or myth. But that does not discredit it, for the old myth is very much truer than history; the myth is the embodiment of a spiritual and universal truth, which unfolds itself down here in many aspects and different phases, and those aspects and phases are called "history." But the myth lies below them all and they are only expressions of the myth. Naturally, people who know nothing of that larger analysis of life have translated all these myths as they might translate, say, *Æsop's Fables.*

They have done so with even less knowledge, because they have less literature of other kinds with which they can compare these symbols and ideas. It is on that point that so much of the difficulty of the translation of ancient books turns. When you come, for instance, to the Hebrew, there is practically no early literature there except the Scriptures of the Jews. The result is that, in translating, they have not a mass of literature with which they can compare the words, and so get a knowledge of the whole content of the words. Hence it has been said of Hebrew that there is no grammar and no lexicon, thus making the whole of it exceedingly uncertain as regards translation.

When you come to Sanskrit, it is not the paucity of the literature which causes difficulties, but the fact that in the early days the entire literature was religious, and therefore you have not the same amount of varied comparison that you have, say in the Greek. Hence for those to whom these languages are foreign, there is a great deal of difficulty in translating them fully and accurately; and because of that, it is of great value that we have the tradition that is embodied in the pandits. It is that which we must have and be familiar with, in order to have a rational and intelligible translation of the old Sanskrit. The Orientalists complain that they cannot use that tradition thus handed down orally from age to age; yet without it a true knowledge of Eastern literature is impossible.

Turn now to another subject about which there is

a good deal of interest—the fact that each of these different worlds in which we live has its own Protector, who is always there watching what is going on. You will remember how the "Silent Watcher" is spoken of in *The Secret Doctrine,* how He is outside the circle of the world, and how He is always there, watching. You will remember how it is pointed out by H. P. B. that He is not taking any active part at all; He is simply there as a Guardian. If it were possible (it always seems an impossible thing to think of) for any error to be made in the working out of that part of the Divine Plan which is in the hands of the four Kumaras, then theoretically He would interfere. That is the whole idea of the Hierarchy; grade upon grade, each standing higher in knowledge and power than the one below it. If any mistake is made by the leader of any grade, then the leader of the next grade above interferes.

You will remember the very strange remark which has been made; I mention it (though I do not understand it) because it illustrates this. It has been said that the Lord Buddha made a mistake. Now that seems to me a very curious phrase to apply in such a case. What is indicated by it, and has sometimes been hinted, is that in His extraordinary love for the world, He gave a little more than the world was ready to receive. That is what is traditionally said to underlie the statement; and therefore Shri Shankaracharya was sent, some eighty years after the Lord Buddha had passed over into Para-Nirvana, in order, as it were, to seal up a little of that for which the world was not yet quite ready, and which might therefore cause a certain amount of harm.

I have sometimes thought that it is possible that the lack of the doctrine of the continuing ego in the Southern Church may possibly have come from the spreading of the Buddhist Religion outside of India among a people who were not familiar with the metaphysic and the cosmogony of Hinduism. In India itself, the stress which the Lord Buddha laid upon conduct, the exquisite simplicity of His teachings (intended to help the ignorant as well as the learned), could not in any way mislead, because all the people knew the underlying Hinduism, and He Himself, being a Hindu, took it for granted. Hence there was no need for Him to emphasize the side of the truths which was so familiar to them. He gave what was wanted at the time for the mass of the people, and thereby changed the whole ethical and religious life of India.

It may be that when the teaching passed on among Fourth Race people, while magnificent in its ethical aspect, the omission of that metaphysical side (so familiar in India) led to a certain amount of materialism in the Southern Church. I have sometimes thought that that may have been what has lain under this traditional phrase. I find myself unable to think of a mistake in connection with the Lord Buddha, and I have some times imagined that it was a wider view which underlay the crude statement.

To Him the temporary materialism was a trifle that might color the ethical value which was so enormously above it. After all it did not so much matter, so long as people were living pure and noble lives under the influence of His ethic, that they should blunder to some extent on the metaphysical questions.

The meaning of the skandhas, and so on, makes very little, if any, practical difference. Any mistake that may have been made by the more ignorant people about such matters would not at all affect the mass of the population in their evolution.

If you take the ordinary Burmese, for instance: they are a simple, gentle, happy type, distinctively Fourth Race, very religious, very charitable, and of the most exquisite moral character. They are the product of the teaching. And if one might venture the suggestion, it may be that in the enormous width of view of such a Being as the Lord Buddha, practical help to evolution may have entirely outweighed the question as to whether their metaphysic was right or wrong.

Metaphysic which depends upon knowledge gained from the senses is always wrong, because it is always partial. You and I may think ourselves very wise in regard to our Theosophical teaching, but I have not the slightest doubt that we are making tremendous blunders over it, and that when we reach the higher stages we shall see how comparatively poor and incompetent were our views of these widespreading and immense truths. It is because of this that we need such complete tolerance. Our view may be true in a very real sense of the word. It is true of as much as we see, but there is so much more that we do not see, which, when it is seen, modifies that view. Hence the need to realize that in putting forward any doctrine, we must always leave the door open for a wider and fuller explanation, which may very much modify the statement that we are making.

In expounding the idea of reincarnation, for instance, we have taught it from the wrong standpoint, from the standpoint of the circumference, from the standpoint of the personality, and of how reincarnation seems to the personality. This causes people to make all sorts of blunders in considering it, because they are all looking at it from this wrong viewpoint. If we transfer ourselves to the center and think of the individuality, think of the higher man himself as the continuing, the incarnating, being, then our view of reincarnation changes enormously. We do not lose the truth we had in the narrower view, but we do see how it is modified, how the proportion and the relationships are all changed. The way we present it will also be different. But to present it in that form to the ordinary mass of people in the West, where it has not yet been received universally, would hinder its acceptance, and so it is put in the more popular form.

That must be true in our own case also. It must be that the Masters put the great truths in a form suited to our limited intelligence, in a form which enables us to assimilate those truths at our stage of understanding. It is exactly the same as in giving food to people. If you fed a baby on the food given to grown-up people, it would choke and die. In fact, one reason for the high mortality of infants is that they are fed wrongly; they are fed on food good for grown-up people but bad for babies. So it is in the matter of truth. We want truth in a form that we can assimilate, so that we can grow up by it, just as the baby wants food in a form that it can assimilate; otherwise it cannot grow. If these great truths came thundering down upon us just as they are, they would crush us and we should be broken up by them. The Masters are wise, being, as it were, educated mothers and not ordinary mothers, and so they are careful in feeding their spiritual babes.

So we get only partial truth. We must all remember that; otherwise there is the danger of building up a new dogmatism in Theosophy, and those who come after us in a generation or two will have the greatest trouble in breaking free from that, just as some of us had in breaking the very narrow conceptions into which we were born. We must not make that difficulty for the future. That is why they call me a "latitudinarian," because I leave plenty of room for people to expand all round. In that way we shall guard our posterity from some of the errors from which we are suffering. I speak of that because I nearly died in breaking my own fetters, and I do not want to have Theosophy fastened down into orthodoxy to harass people three or four generations from now.

Let us return for a moment again to this Protector or Guardian. He is called a Tathagata or a Dhyan-Chohan, and in the Buddhist books you have very many of them. If you think of the word Tathagata as applying only to those whom we call Buddhas, you will be very much perplexed, because we find so very many of Them and They seem everywhere. You wonder where They belong, and what office They fill. But when you realize that every world, and all of these divisions that we call planes, has a "Watcher," and that every one of those has a Tathagata (which, after all, only means "He who follows in the footsteps of

His predecessors''), then you will understand why these large numbers are given in the books.

But He is there to protect and watch over, and not not to interfere with, the normal course of evolution marked out by the Divine Will. Our bit of it in the plan of the world is marked out by our Ishvara, and given over to the Head of the Hierarchy. That must not be interfered with; and if there is a danger of any force coming which is strong enough to interfere with or suspend that law, then it is that the Dhyan-Chohan or the Tathagata steps in at once, puts things right, and prevents the interference which would mar the harmonious working out of the plan.

* * * * *

A perpetually interesting question is that of the survival of the early Christian Mysteries. You will find that in the Roman Catholic Church there are many ancient traditions which have been preserved and handed down from the earliest times, when the Mysteries were still in the Church. Each great religion, of course, had its own Mysteries, and you know how the early Fathers of the Church speak of the ''Mysteries of Jesus,'' the Mysteries that the Master Jesus had given to those whom He instructed. By analogy there can be no reasonable doubt that those contained the whole of the great occult truths.

Parts of these have certainly been handed down by tradition in the Roman Catholic Church. I always think it possible that among the very highest members of that Church there may be a secret teaching; there is no doubt that in the library of the Vatican there are a number of secret books which are never allowed to go outside a very, very small circle. These act as intermediaries and give a certain amount of occult teaching to some of the great Orders of the Roman Catholic Church.

The Jesuit Order is one of them, and that is the reason why H. P. B. showed such a very strong antagonism to it. It has a knowledge of certain occult facts which it utilizes to obtain an influence over the minds of human beings, and, as you know, that idea of controlling the human will by occult means is distinctly the way of the black magician. I do not mean by this that every Jesuit is on the road to become a black magician; that would be most unfair, for among the Jesuit Order there are a number of the most spiritual and noble men that you can imagine. It is a marvelous Order for its utter self-sacrifice and extraordinary activity of life. But the higher people in it, the rulers in it, have this knowledge. Some of it they pass on, but in a form which would not strike the ordinary Jesuit as having anything wrong about it. Of course he would not inquire whether it is wrong or not, when it comes to him through a superior officer.

There lies the danger. We, on the other hand, are always told to follow our conscience. While it is true that a warning on this point has been given somewhat caustically: "Take care that your conscience is not the conscience of a fool" (the remark of a prelate in the time of Charles I to one of the Nonconformist people whom he was trying to terrify into conformity), still it is best to follow your conscience whether it is the conscience of a fool or not. After all, if you have only made yourself up to that stage of folly, you must act according to the stage you have created for yourself. You cannot blame the person who acts according to his nature; and it will take him some time to alter that nature. That is another stage of tolerance. If a person acts wrongly or foolishly it is because he has made himself that way, and his action is the outcome of his nature. He ought to change himself, and you should try to help him, but he must really do it for himself.

Hence in Theosophy we always say: Judge morality by your conscience; do not do a thing if to you it seems wrong. The Jesuit does not say that; he has to do what his superior tells him to do—to be "as a staff in the hand of the superior." His whole movement is rooted in that. That brings out some extraordinary virtues; but it also has dangers, and it is the dangerous side that has led to the exclusion of the Jesuits from certain continental countries, because they become dangerous to the State. and the State never knows whom it has to deal with, for the reason that they blindly obey their superiors.

The principal point that I want to mention to you, with regard to this occult teaching, is the power of thought. The knowledge is becoming now fairly widespread, but some time ago it was not widely known. But the Jesuits were taught it, and they used it whenever they had a mission anywhere; that is, when they went out. to preach Roman Catholic doctrines. On those occasions one or two people would go down to study the physical appearance of the place of meeting. Then they would map out the district in which they were going to work, and carry the map back to their headquarters. Then they go into a dark room—dark because concentration is easier in the dark; a certain number of them form a little circle and hold each other's hands, so as to become magnetically joined. Then they fix their minds upon one single thing, one of the Roman Catholic doctrines that they are going to preach; and they think of themselves as in this particular place where their work is to be done. Then they think of one of themselves as preaching (the whole of the art of visualization is taught to them) and they fill the whole mental atmosphere of that particular locality with this one thought. Then they go out and preach it.

You see at once the effect of that on the mass of the people they address. Their brains have been played upon by this thought-image and the whole ground has been carefully prepared; hence they are much more receptive. Many more of them come and listen; and many more of them will be impressed with the teaching that is given. It is in that fashion that this occult force is utilized.

I cannot tell you how far that goes, because, not being in that Order, I do not know its secrets. This I happen to know, because I have been told by a Jesuit that this is the way they work. Of course, it does make them, in a sense, a dangerous element if the force is turned to evil. If it were turned to the spreading of some evil thought, not a religious doctrine, then it might do a great deal of harm; and one can hardly tell how far that goes in those cases where they have been reported as entering into a conspiracy against the State, or even to dispose of a person who is in their way.

It is the fact that they act under orders blindly that has caused their exclusion from many European States, in some ways to the disadvantage of the people, because the ordinary Jesuit is a very admirable person, a person of absolute self-sacrifice and unselfishness. The Jesuit missionaries have been the noblest missionaries that have ever gone out into the world. They live a most ascetic life, they give themselves absolutely to what they are doing, and they are full of love. Some of the great saints of the Roman Catholic Church came from that Order.

If they turn to evil, then they finally become the type of person who would be thrown out of the world's evolution, just as the black magician who has gone too far wrong will be thrown out of the world and will be got rid of. Something of that kind is going on in this present War; some of the quite irredeemable people, who are participating in this great struggle, will be thrown out and will pass into Avichi, to wait there until some future planet is evolved, when they will again begin their evolution.

* * * * *

You know how often the question is asked: Is any given life-period a fixed period? If by that question is meant: Does a person die out of the physical body at a fixed time? the answer is: No; other causes may be brought in. There are certain causes which work toward that point; several times in the course of a person's life-period his past karma brings him to what you may call a rather critical stage. Upon the force then brought to bear upon him will depend whether he passes out of the physical body at that time or not. But the whole life under physical conditions is a fixed period, and if he passes out of earthly life before that period is fulfilled on the physical plane, he has to live on for the remainder of it under what you may call partly-earth-life conditions in the astral world. His physical body has been struck away before its life-period is over. But the normal period after death only begins when that earthly life-period is exhausted; that is the point you have to remember. Here in India you are very often asked that question, because there are a number of verses in the Shastras which imply that death only comes at a certain time. Normally death does so come. You remember the verse in one of the books: that before the period comes "a lance will not kill; when it comes a blade of grass is enough to kill." The ordinary person reading that will naturally think only of the physical body. If you take it in a little wider sense and take the blade of grass as a symbol, then you will have the entirely true conception that, when the time comes, the smallest cause will bring about the striking away of the physical body. If that time has not come, then even a violent cause—the lance—cannot alter the life-period; but still it may strike away the physical body.

People sometimes get puzzled over this matter and they ask a mass of questions which lead to very undesirable results. For instance, they say: "Oh, well, if a person's life-period is fixed, if the death hour is fixed, what is the good of nursing him or of bringing a doctor? Leave him alone; if he dies, it will show that it is his time to die; if it is his karma to live, he will live." And you do occasionally get cases where that is actually carried out. Now that is a serious mistake; you are bound to do what you can, for at a critical period you may change the result by your present activities. Yet people sometimes refrain from those activities because of the mistaken idea that the physical life-period is fixed; and it leads to undesirable results.

The fact is that the period of life under physical conditions *is* fixed; the period of striking off the physical body is *not* fixed. At one point or another death may come. There will be times when, because of the karma, death cannot be averted, but there may be other periods when an added force may turn it away like any other kind of karma. There are points that are certain, and there are those that may be varied by exertion.

This illustrates the important fact that because right conduct is so enormously important to people's happiness and progress, it is necessary to use great discrimination in telling them things which, while in themselves true, may mislead them and make them act in a wrong way.

CHAPTER VI

AFTER-DEATH EXPERIENCES OF SUICIDES

What of the after-death experiences of those who have committed suicide or who die by accident? In the second class, there is a very great variety. In the first, there is the definite living out of the life-period; that means, of course, the period for the working out of the karma of that life, and for that the body is practically built. The body is made for a certain time, to last through a certain period, and during that period the karma selected for working out should be exhausted.

You probably know from your general reading that there are possibilities, especially where the ego is more developed, where some power of choice can be exercised with regard to bringing in karma which is not really quite ripe for exhaustion, or of putting off karma, retarding it, which should have been worked out in that particular life. That is to say that here, as everywhere else, if you bring in a new force you alter the result.

That is one point you should keep clearly in mind in all these discussions on karma—that you are dealing only with a law of nature, and that where you bring in some other condition the result must inevitably change. It is because people forget this, that they become so confused about karma, thinking that they cannot do anything and that they are helpless. Karma is always a thing which can be modified according to the introduction of a new force, exactly like any other law in nature.

There are cases with regard to premature death, where an opportunity for such death, offered by an "accident," has been taken by the choice of the ego; suppose that sudden death was in a man's karma, the paying of some debt where he had caused the sudden death of somebody else. It might be that no opportunity had occurred during several lives for the exhaustion of that particular part of his karma, and that it was hindering his progress.

Now the karma which is chosen by the Lipika for any particular life-period must be what is called "congruous"; there must be present the persons who were concerned in the causes of which this karma is the effect. It may very well be that for a given life, say of any of us, some of the people with whom we have been connected in the past may be away in the heaven world, and their time for coming back has not yet arrived; under those conditions the karma in connection with them has to be put off. It cannot be worked out until they are on the physical plane, and they cannot be dragged out of the heaven world until they have worked out the whole of their past experience into faculty. You will see at once that to shorten a person's work in that world, so that he has not had time to work up the whole of his past experience into the faculty with which he should be reborn, would be an exceedingly difficult and awkward thing to do—in fact, an unfair and unjust thing to do.

But the mere putting off of some karmic results

that have a connection with that man is a trivial thing; it is merely a matter of time, which does not count, and which is very easily changed by Those who regulate the working of the law. Under these conditions, then, you might have an opportunity of a sudden death, say by a railway accident or an earthquake, a flood or a shipwreck; any of these things in which a large number of people are gathered together who have to die at that time; this is always the case where there is an artificial catastrophe like a shipwreck, or a natural one like an earthquake. A number of people will be guided to that particular ship or that particular place by the Devas, in order that they may have that particular part of their karmic debt paid.

If an ego desired to work that off for any particular reason in his own mind, he might be given the opportunity, he might be guided to go aboard that ship, or to go into a particular train, and in that fashion, choosing a sudden death, he would pay his own debt. If he happened to be an advanced ego, round whom this was hanging as a kind of shackle or fetter, preventing his going on, this is a thing he would be apt to do. Such cases very often occur in these so-called "accidental" deaths.

You may have noticed, however, that in these accidents there are often some very extraordinary "escapes," as they are called. A man, perhaps the only man, will escape from shipwreck, or something like that; he, you may at once know, is a man who has not death of that kind in his own karma, or else is not advanced enough to take advantage of that opportunity, if it were in his karma. Those cases, then, will mingle with the accidents.

Let us now take the case of suicide, which is an entirely different thing. We shall exclude for the moment the suicide which is deliberately chosen for the sake of some great good to others. But the ordinary suicide is committed from a momentary despair, or from a shock which the person is not strong enough to bear, a sudden misfortune coming upon him from some wrong action which he fears will be discovered and the penalty of which he wishes to escape. So, putting aside the exception which I have mentioned, suicide is from either weakness or cowardice. It is the deliberate or the hurried action of the man who is trying to get out of a trouble and escape from it.

Yet he cannot escape from it. When he has struck away his body, he is wide awake on the other side of death, exactly the same man he was a moment before, except that his body is thrown off; no more changed than if he had merely taken off his coat. The result of his losing the physical body is that his capacity for suffering is very much increased. He is subject to the same forces as those which may have driven him to suicide. There is, however, one peculiarity in relation to it—that he generally goes through in "imagination," as we call it (which is the most real thing of all), all that led up to the point when he killed himself, and that is repeated over and over again.

A great deal of the suffering depends upon that. The thing which drove him to suicide was mental or emotional, as the case may be. He has not got rid either of his mind or his emotions. All the part of him that drove him to suicide is there; it was not a mere bodily action. The result of that is that he has still in him everything which made him commit the act; the consequence of this is that he keeps on committing it, going through the whole of the trouble that drove him up to the final act. Of course, that is suffering of an exceedingly acute kind. Hence the horror with which suicide has been regarded by all people who understand it; also the reason why almost all religions have forbidden it. If you speak to the ordinary Hindu, you will find that he has the strongest feeling against suicide as being wrong.

That has come out in a very curious form in the law in the West; for if a man has attempted to commit suicide and has failed, he is brought before a magistrate and is subject to punishment; this seems a remarkable proceeding, because a magistrate should really have nothing to do with the case. It is almost absurd to punish a man by a physical law for an attempt to end his own life. Still more strange is the result if two people have determined to commit suicide together, as, for instance, two lovers, or a husband and wife, who do not wish to part even in death, but who are driven by some great trouble into killing themselves. If only one of them happens to die, the law brings the other up on a charge of murder, which seems a very clumsy and unjust proceeding. Such laws are due to want of occult knowledge.

The working out of the natural law on the other side of death is a perfect sequence: it goes on naturally from what happened here. It is inevitable, and that is of course the great mark of all natural law. While the penalty of the artificial law is itself artificial and may be changed, the penalty, or rather the sequence, in the natural law is inevitable.

The karmic penalty of the crime committed is the injury to the moral nature. The artificial penalty may be the scaffold, or imprisonment for a long time, or it may be any other penalty that the legislative authority chooses to attach to it. But the karmic penalty is always the inevitable result of what a man has done. The karmic penalty of a lie, for instance, is that a man becomes less truthful and there is more tendency in him to tell another lie. In all these cases it is inevitable, and the result must follow.

That curious automatic effect, the repeating of a thing over and over again in Kama-loka, is also a characteristic of the murderer when he passes over, whether the murder is found out or not. Of course, if he is found out and hanged, then it takes place in rapid sequence. He goes back to the origin of the thought of murder in his own mind, the causes which made him determine on it. Then he passes stage by stage through all the mental phases that preceded the murder. I remember one case that was publicly mentioned at the time, that of the murderer of either Lincoln or Garfield, Presidents of the United States. After death the murderer went on committing this murder over and over again, with everything that led up to it.

In studying people, when we were conducting our various investigations with regard to post-mortem states, we found similar cases very frequently. That is one of the ways in which the savage learns that murder is wrong. The savage kills without thinking. It cannot be said to be much of a crime, so far as he is concerned, but it is important that he should learn that murder is a thing he must not do. And so, in the post-mortem life, he has a short suffering of this kind, short because there was very little mental effort behind it, and because there was merely the sudden emotion, leading to the committing of that act. That is part of the useful instruction which helps in the evolution of the savage: he learns the thing is wrong by finding it works out painfully for him. But, of course, those who have grown up from childhood with the conviction that their past lives have made them what they are would suffer for a very much longer period if they committed a similar offense.

The folly in suicide is that people erroneously expect to escape life, and then they find themselves still alive. That is the futility of the whole thing. It is so silly. It is important now and then to lay a little stress on this in speaking to ordinary people in a lecture: to emphasize the folly of it more than the wrong of it. It is more likely to be effective, for sometimes the wrong is comparatively small, but the folly is always great. Suicide depends chiefly upon ignorance: let people be convinced that they cannot escape, that the results of action are inevitable, and that will work upon their minds when there is a sudden impulse to suicide from the desire to escape. They cannot escape; and if to that you add the fact that they suffer there more than here because they are working in subtler matter, in which the impact of feeling is stronger in its effect upon consciousness (because less of it is wasted in moving that matter, the matter being very much lighter), you may in that way produce a very considerable effect upon their minds.

I have sometimes found that to be the case with

drunkards: where you explain the facts along these rational lines, where you show them the inevitableness of the suffering, where you can emphasize the increase of the suffering, you can occasionally supply a motive which will help them to keep back from drink.

The suicide is very apt to turn up at a spiritualistic séance. Remember that he has not, by this act of suicide, broken away completely from his higher principles. But if he does not accept the results and act upon good advice (as he may be induced to do by the people who help him on the other side of death, and who will point out to him that these are the inevitable consequences of his action, and that it is best to take them patiently and quietly), he often comes to regret his rash act and to attempt to regain a hold upon life by wrong means.

In Kama-loka, the land of intense desires (intense for the reason I have just given you), he can gratify his earthly yearnings through a living proxy and, if he does so, then at the expiration of what would have been the natural term of his life (when the normal conditions would have come), the Monad generally loses him for ever. That is, he breaks away, and then he has to go back to the very beginning of evolution because the permanent atoms have been torn away.

To all this there is an exception in the case of the suicide which has been committed from a noble motive. This is rare, but there are cases. I remember H. P. B. mentioning that the suicide of the Czar Nicholas of Russia, just before the end of the Crimean War, was such a case. It was not known publicly that he had committed suicide, but as a matter of fact he had killed himself. His motive in killing himself was to put an end to the war. His life was an obstacle to that. His people were greatly devoted to him, for there was in the past a great devotion on the part of the mass of the Russian people to their Czar: they looked upon him as their father. They would not consent to stop the war at the cost of his humiliation; they wanted to go on fighting on the vague chance that they might win in time, and thus save the Czar from the humiliation of defeat. He saw, as I suppose most of the people of more knowledge saw, that the defeat was inevitable because they were overmatched. He determined, therefore, to kill himself, so as to remove from his people the motive for continuing the war, and so save additional bloodshed and violence.

There you have a distinct act of self-sacrifice. He did not kill himself to escape something for himself, but to save the suffering which his people were enduring. It was an act of love and self-sacrifice, and the result of that to him was exceedingly beneficial. It was not regarded at all as a suicide, although physically it was a suicide: it was taken as a great act of moral sacrifice, similar to that of a man who plunges into a burning house to save a woman, or child, or anybody else who is there. In a sense he is committing suicide, if he dies by it; at any rate, he is willing to take the risk, and because of that he kills himself. Such an act is not suicide in the ordinary sense, and it does not cause suffering after death. It is an act of self-sacrifice which quickens evolution, and does not retard it.

Quite frequently the suicides and those who have died by accident desire to get into touch with the living. If they are left alone, they cannot do this, because there is a barrier between them and the ordinary world which cannot be broken on their side. But the medium is an exception: the medium, by a peculiar physical constitution, by the slack connection between the dense and the etheric parts of the physical body, acts as a kind of bridge. He, the very commonplace and undeveloped medium, opens a door to communication on the two lower sub-planes of the astral; and, opening that door, he may either give some of his material to these materializing ghosts, or he may himself be overshadowed by them and made their tool. Those are the two possibilities.

If the medium has somebody protecting him on the other side, then these will be kept away from him. And that is why W. T. Stead, who knew a good deal about these conditions, guarded his "bureau" very carefully. His deceased friend Julia, and some of their friends on the astral plane, made a kind of wall around the bureau. The proper conditions were made by the fact that only a certain class of people were allowed to come to it: only people who were rather above the average in goodness, pure-minded and earnest people (not necessarily intellectual), who lived well and thought well and had aspirations. Those were the only people whom he admitted.

He did not bring in anybody who would be an attraction to the lower kind of person on the astral plane. Then the astral friends made a protecting wall round it, and so the very best conditions were obtained. He had some very satisfactory results.

But in the ordinary circle, where people come in by paying so much (half a crown, or five or ten shillings), there is no check at all as to the kind of persons who are admitted. As these meetings are usually held in the evenings, the people who attend are very often the merely curious, and come for fun and amusement. They may come in after a heavy dinner, after eating meat and drinking wine, and so they bring with them very bad conditions.

The result on the unfortunate medium is very, very bad; there is also the possibility that anyone who is there of a low type, whose passions and character are bad, may attract to himself one of these entities of similar tendencies, who is naturally drawn to such séances from the astral world. Suppose, then, that one of these lower ghosts should attach himself to the astral body of a person in the séance, having had the opportunity by materializing himself (by drawing the necessary particles from the body of the medium) and then of making this link with this special person, then he would obsess him, influence him, fill his mind with bad thoughts. The few cases of this kind that I have come across (fortunately I have not come across many) have been of the most distressing character to the mediumistic person who, without being evil in any way, was receptive, and so taken hold of, or of persons who had strong passions and had them intensified by going to a séance.

In these facts you have the reason for H. P. B.'s strong denunciation of séances. In the early days, while she was writing, they were to be found everywhere. She utilized them to some extent herself when she first came, because the Spiritualists were the only people she could reach, and some of them in America and England were, like Stainton Moses, of a high kind, people who were fit to come into occult training. She tried to reach people of that type. Then she separated herself entirely from Spiritualists, because of the mischief that was being done to large numbers of people in America and England, and began strongly to denounce them, and so she drew against herself the very great wrath of the Spiritualists. But she felt that the amount of comfort which a few people might derive from going to the better kind of séance was out of all proportion to the harm that was done to the people who went to the inferior séances.

Some of the better kind were carried on by Theosophists for a considerable period, and remarkable results were obtained; but so far as the public was concerned, the attitude was adopted of going entirely against them. Nowadays the matter is not of the same importance; most of the séances are held by circles which have learned the dangers, and are very much more particular about who enters them, and so at the present time they do very little harm.

Persons who have not had much evil in their minds, and who are killed by sudden accident, live consciously on the astral plane; they have no recollection of the accident, and move among their family, their friends, and old familiar scenes. From our standpoint their life may be called dreamy, but from their standpoint it is more real than the life they have left, and they are quite happy.

The first thing they notice after a time is that they cannot converse with their friends during their waking life. For some time they think they can, and they do not understand why their friends do not notice them; but the lack of notice makes them realize that they cannot communicate, and that they have passed through death into a different condition. What is daytime to the "living" is night to the "dead," because then they cannot communicate with their living friends; but our night is their day, because then their friends are liberated during the sleep of their physical bodies, and then they can communicate with them and be happy.

The average person, he who has a good many bad thoughts and some good ones, ought of all people to keep away from the séance, because there is just enough in him to attract, not the very worst, but a very undesirable kind of dweller on the astral plane. The result of the séance to him is that by giving to these people an opportunity of acting vicariously (he being the medium for it, while the other is the motive power), he helps the man who is on the astral plane to keep on making a good deal of karma. Now Kamaloka ought to be, for the normal man, one of the worlds of effects; it is a world of effects where he should work out certain parts of his karma. If he goes to a séance under these conditions, he is apt to be making new karma with other people. He is more responsible than the living man who is the object of his impulse, and the bulk of the karma is made by the impulse, by him who starts it, not by the agent who carries it out. The latter shares it, but not nearly to so great an extent. So for this man the world of effects is thus turned into a world of causes, and very possibly of worse causes than he would have started if left to himself, because the ordinary medium is a very unintellectual person, who is apt to do things badly and poorly.

CHAPTER VII

BYWAYS OF EVOLUTION

People who had passed out of this life, who had gone on to Devachan, are, as you know, drawn back again to earth-life by their own desires, by trishna, the thirst for sentient existence. It is worth while to remember—for the sake of general knowledge perhaps—that trishna may be of different kinds and, as one of the Upanishats points out, a man is born in the world to which his desires lead him.

Now it is quite possible that during any special earth-life, a man's desires may lead him, not into Devachan, but into some other world—a point that is not very often considered. Supposing that he wishes that growth of the whole nature, the working up of experience into faculty, which takes place in Devachan, then he will naturally go thither. But suppose we take the case of one of the less developed yogis, say in India. *There* is a man who has deliberately killed out the desires which belong to this particular world. He has realized that the world is transitory, that it is hardly worth while to take very much trouble to remain in it, and perhaps his life before he went into Yoga was one of unhappiness and disappointment. He might have reached that form of vairagya—the "burning-ground vairagya" — which does not lead to Liberation in the strict sense of the term, but only to a very partial liberation.

Supposing that that has happened, and that the man has given all his years to meditation and killed out, for the time being only (but he does not know that), the desire for anything that this world can give him. He passes away. What is to bring him back, or whither will he be brought? He has extinguished for the time being the particular trishna which would bring him back to this world. Then there is nothing which should bring him back, because it is desire which guides him to any particular world.

There are many cases of this sort in which a man passes into a loka (a world) which is not permanent, but in which he may remain practically for ages. And that is obtained by one of the forms of vairagya. There are a number of those other worlds, connected very often with the worship of a particular Divine form, connected with special kinds of meditation, and so on, and a man may pass into one of those and may remain there for a quite indefinite time. Ultimately he has to come back to a world, either this world if it is still going on, or a world similar to this, where he can take up his evolution at the point at which it was dropped. But it might be worth your while just to remember that possibility, because it has to do with cases which you might be asked to explain,.

Supposing that you get a man who is of average goodness, who is not distinguished by any great self-sacrifice, any great desire for the service of others (things which are the marks of the real spiritual life, of the growth of spirituality, because they are the recognition—whether consciously or not on this plane—of the unity of life, and that recognition of the One is what we mean by the word "spirituality"); such a man has not reached a high spiritual level at all. He is quite an average person with no particular intellectual or moral qualities of a remarkable kind.

He is clearly not fit for "Liberation," as we know it; that is, he is not fit to enter upon the Path, let alone to reach the Fifth of the great Initiations, which gives what we call Moksha, or Liberation. What then is to become of him? There is nothing to bring him back here, because he has killed that out for the time. Where is he to go? What will happen to him? He obtains a form of Moksha; he does stay away from this world in a condition in which he is quite happy, but in which he is of no particular use either to himself or to anybody else.

There are cases where a man has gone a considerable way along the Path and where he may pass away to some form of Moksha which is lower than the complete thing; then he may be very useful there. He may have reached a stage of meditation in which his mental powers are of very great value; he may then be able to influence the world, not consciously. but by his meditation in some other world he may help in that great stream of mental and spiritual energy which is drawn upon by the Masters for Their work in the world. You all realize that there is such a reservoir of spiritual force; in the highest sense it is kept full of energy by Those whom we speak of as the Nirmanakayas, very lofty Beings; it is They who, as it were, fill that reservoir for the use of the worlds. But others may contribute to it, though in a very much lesser fashion; and you might have a man who had made considerable progress, who wished to remain in the condition of meditation, and to make that his way of serving the world. And he can do it.

You ought to try gradually to realize the enormous power that you have over your own futures; that you are not drifting about on the sea of existence, but that you have begun to put your hand on the rudder of your own particular ship, and that you can very, very largely control your own future and your methods of working.

Suppose, then, that such a man, who has reached a considerable point of intellectual power through meditation, through concentration, is able to use that power in meditation, and suppose that that is the best expression of his service to the world. Then his wish to be of service would take him off to a world in which he could work along that particular line. It would be a world about the level of the causal body, the higher regions of the mental plane. He could inhabit such a world, live there literally for ages, and be of use, because he would be pouring out this stream of concentrated thought for the helping of others, and so helping to supply this reservoir of spiritual power.

That is one possibility, and I think it would be a good thing if all of you could realize these very large and varied possibilities that lie before the human Spirit. We are so apt to limit our thought of evolution, and of rest from evolution, to what you may call the normal, average way, running round and round and round the three worlds, then entering on the Path reaching the stage of Jivanmukti, and then the seven great Paths that branch out from it. We do not always remember that in connection with each plane there are numerous lokas or places, which for the moment we may call worlds, in which there are very varied possibilities to meet the very varied developments of the individual.

While there is no particular need that you should go carefully and thoroughly into the subject, I think it is well that you should recognize this fact, for it may often happen, especially here in India, that you may be asked questions as to what happens to these people who have given up the world, who are leading these very ascetic lives, who have not reached any point of development which makes them really fit for the work of the Hierarchy, the higher work in the helping of the world, but who do contribute, some of them, their own share to the helping of the world.

Others of them below that level simply have an exceedingly blissful existence for ages, and then come back again to some world in the same stage as the one they left. There are these very varied possibilities outside the ordinary run. Nature is so full of possibilities that she meets every individualized creature just according to his needs; so that that which is best for the individual, by the choice of the Monad (which is the dominating force always), she will meet by the provision in this boundless realm of hers of that which suits the choice of that particular Monad.

I just allude to this, because I have been glancing over that phrase of the Upanishats that refers to these many worlds into which men go. And I would say to those of you who do not know the major Upanishats well, that a careful reading of them would add enormously to your knowledge. Most of you should now be able to read them with an intelligence, an insight, which is not generally brought to bear upon them, and in that way you might learn from them very much wider views of the world than for the most part are entertained.

Let us now turn to the subject of the "elementary." Remember that that word is specifically used for the human being who has dropped his physical body at death, and who is still in all the rest of the bodies, except the etheric, as the physical includes the etheric. He has dropped that, but he has all the rest of the bodies, and he lives in the world which belongs to the lowest of them; that is, he is living on the astral plane. As long as he is living there he is technically called an "elementary" (not "elemental," which is on a different line). I may just, perhaps, remind you, in passing, that when he has thrown off some of those concentric shells of astral matter in which his astral body is normally rearranged after death, and when he has drawn himself out of those and is in the finer levels of the astral, then that which he leaves behind is called the "shell."

You want to remember those little distinctions carefully, so that you may follow H. P. B. in her statements, because she frequently talks of "shells," and she means, by those, these cast-off remnants of the astral man which have life enough in them to keep together for a time, but which the man has left. He is no longer there. The great mark of the "shells" is that they continually repeat the same thing; if you are familiar with Spiritualism you will easily recognize the "shell." The "shell" comes out in automatic writing or through materialization, when it repeats the old things over and over again, such as: "I am very happy," "I am pleased to see you," "It is a very beautiful world," and so on; there is no information given, nothing that is worth anything. A very large part of such communications comes from the "shells."

Spiritualists, not understanding H. P. B.'s nomenclature, have believed that she meant that the word "shell" applied to everybody who is on the other side, and so a great deal of misconception has arisen and they have attacked her quite unnecessarily, asserting that she said that all the communications came from "shells." But that is not so: she used the word "shell" in a specific way—those still-vivified, automatic, denser parts of the astral body, which in the rearrangement after death have been shed by the man, who has gone on to the higher parts of the astral world, and has left behind on the lower these remnants which are most available for the medium.

In a previous talk I explained to you the condition of the person who was the victim of an accident, or who had committed suicide. Take a person who kills himself. He has antedated the hour for which his mortal bodies were made. Now mortal bodies, remember, include three: physical, astral, and mental. Those are made by karma for a particular length of life. That idea causes confusion sometimes. There is what I have called the "life-period"—a particular phrase to cover that idea; I have used it to indicate the particular periods for which these three bodies are built.

Of course, that applies most to the physical body. That is built for a particular number of years; it is meant to last so many years, and that is according to the karma which is chosen to exhaust itself in that particular body. If the man lives out the life for which his physical body has been built, then he will have worn out that "ripe" karma, which he was meant to wear out in this particular body. That is, of course, the arrangement of the Lords of Karma, who select the ripe karma, and of the Devas, who build according to the mold which they have been given; then the building elemental, being given the mold of that, builds according to it and shapes it for a particular life-period. That is the normal condition.

You know roughly, I think, how the karma is chosen—that which is sufficiently congruous to be worked out at a particular age of the world, in a particular country, a particular family, and a particular environment of people and circumstances. It is a very complicated thing, if you think of it for a moment. You have made all sorts of karma with a special set of people; you are making it now with the people around you. As a matter of fact that will, for most of us, work out more easily than usual because of the peculiar conditions of the time; we shall be brought back here quickly, so that a large part of that working-out will come easily.

But take an ordinary person not being born in a transitional period, such as we are born in now, but one of the longer periods of evolution that come between these periods of transition. He makes for himself a network of karma with certain individuals; but each of these individuals has his own karma: one of them may be staying for a long time in Devachan, another a short time; one has to be born in one country, another in a different one. You can see how varied these conditions are.

It is the work of the Lipika to choose out of all these

interwoven webs of karma so much as can be lived out in a particular body; to choose the country which will be suitable. This is one of the important things, but one of lesser importance because the individual can be moved to another country if necessary. It is important because a person has a karma in the special country in which he is born. But you may say this: his physical body is the one thing that matters in so far as his country is concerned; his body is made suitable for the work he is to do, but it may not affect the individual's personal karma so much. He can still move about from one country to another, because he is what we call a free agent, even though this free agent is moved about so very much by the Devas.

One of you born on the other side of the world may come over here to India, so that you may contact a number of people whose karma has brought them to India for a time; you may also go elsewhere to meet other people, and so you can meet a great many people with whom you have to work out karma. You can see how if a person travels a great deal in different countries, he will be able to exhaust a great deal of karma, because he comes across the people whom he met in previous lives and with whom he has made karma. So he can pay his karma with them, and in that way exhaust it.

But there will be a larger number of the people with whom he has made karmic ties that he cannot meet in a particular life. All those are held over; he has to meet them at some other future time. Those that he will meet in this life-period are the important ones in his karma. He ought to be able to work out the karmic ties which are put down for him in his chart; it is, as it were, said to him: "These are the people you ought to meet; these are the countries you ought to go to; these are the ties you ought to exhaust, and your body is given to you for that purpose."

But suppose a man kills his physical body; he has cut himself off from the working out of those ties, and a mass of ripe karma that he ought to have exhausted remains there, so to speak, in a state of suspension. What should he do? He is at a terrible disadvantage. He has made it difficult by committing suicide; he has refused to work out the karma; he has escaped his karma by cutting off his body which is necessary for working it out. Suppose he has injured a man very much in a past life and that injury is to return to him by (to take a common case) some very great financial loss which ruins him. That might very well happen. If the man is a knower of karma, he will take it quietly and say: "Very well, I have made this karma and I will get rid of it; let me exhaust it, so that I shall not have to meet it again."

But suppose he is an ignorant man, who knows nothing about it, and who sees ruin all about him and has not the courage to face it; he says: "I'll get out of it by killing myself." Of course he cannot kill *himself;* he can kill only his *body.* But the disadvantage is that he cannot work out that karma properly. He is thrown on to the astral plane, surrounded by the circumstances which led him to kill himself. And there lies the suffering for him: those circumstances keep on repeating themselves.

If he has any claims on any person who is more highly developed, or if he has any claims on a Deva, as many people may have for services rendered in the past, then there is a possibility that opens out to him. That more developed person, or Deva, may come to him on the astral plane and may explain to him the conditions of things; he has earned the right to that help. If, then, strength enough can be awakened in him to face this, he may anyhow, under circumstances of greatly increased difficulty, work out a very large part of that karma.

I doubt if he can work out the whole of his karma; he can, however, work out a very large part of it. You may say: "How?" Suppose he says to himself: "Well, there's the man who has injured me most; who has driven me to suicide. I will remain near him and help him in every possible way I can." That would be one way of getting rid of a good deal of it. He works for that man's welfare in every possible way that he can work for it on the astral plane, and he can do a great deal. He wards off dangers, he brings about fortunate conditions, and so on. That would be an exceptionally favorable case, in which the man owes a karmic debt to another which he can repay in this way. He will thus help this man until he has exhausted, as far as practicable, the bad karma which led to this catastrophe in his own life. This instance will serve to show the kind of way in which it can be done.

But there is a special difficulty to be met. There is the desire for physical existence, this trishna which is still in him, and which brought him back to rebirth. That is still a thirst, which on the astral plane has become, not an enjoyment, as it may be here by being satisfied, but a craving which he cannot satisfy and which therefore becomes a torment. What is he to do as regards that? What he will do, if he is ignorant, is to try to satisfy it, and that is where the danger of the medium comes in.

The medium helps to awaken and develop this thirst, because the medium gives the possibility of gratifying the thirst in an illegitimate way, that is, a way which is contrary to the law. The result is that the man makes worse karma, and keeps on making it. The medium gives him the opportunity of talking with people here, coming into touch with them and gratifying himself in very many different ways. And there lies the great responsibility of the medium: he or she becomes a channel for these communications, and any elementaries in the vicinity, who have either committed suicide or who have died a violent death, and who are full of this trishna, or thirst for sentient physical existence, will crowd around that medium.

Of course, there are cases where people have a considerable amount of knowledge, or where they are connected with people on the other side who have knowledge, where all this undesirable crowd will be kept away from the medium. You may have noticed in some of Mr. Stead's statements that he spoke of the guardians who acted in connection with his séances. That is quite true, there are those who act as guardians in special cases where the medium is of pure life, where the motives are good, and where, though there may be an ignorance of *post-mortem* conditions, there is no undesirable wish on the part of the medium, and therefore that medium has a certain claim to protection. Then there will be a certain number of these more developed people on the astral plane, who will protect that particular medium. And you will notice in the case of Mr. Stead, who was helped very much, that he would not take strange people into his spiritualistic circle; he sometimes tried to get answers for strangers, but he would not allow them to come into his circle.

Mr. Stead had, for his circle, a certain number of carefully chosen people who lived very carefully and who were good, religious people, willing to subject themselves to certain restrictions for the sake of doing this particular work; and those were the people who made his circle. The result was that he did come into touch with people on the astral plane of the more desirable kind, a large number of people who wanted to get into touch with their friends; and so he helped a great many. Without saying whether it was altogether wholesome or not, one can at least say that it was done under good conditions, and it was nearer the old way of communication in the days when the Devas were very closely connected with human beings by all the various rituals that were used in the older religions, in order that that touch might be maintained in the best possible way. That time is returning; hence the prevalence of Spiritualism.

In fact, ceremonial aims at that. If you take the ceremonies, the old ceremonies, of Hinduism—not the modern ones—of Zoroastrianism, of Christianity, and of the old dead religions, the Egyptian, the Greek, the Roman and others, you will notice that in all of them there were what we call "Mysteries." The outer ceremonies on the physical plane put people into a certain touch with the Mysteries, which were carried on by the more advanced people of the religion, so that they formed a kind of second circle all around, who reaped, through their ceremonial, benefits from the Mysteries which were being carried on by people with more knowledge.

This is put very definitely in the writings of Origen, the great Christian teacher. He points out that the Church, the ordinary assembly of Christian people, cannot exist healthily without the presence of Gnostics, or Knowers. The Gnostics, or Knowers, were those who were participants in what were called the "Mysteries of Jesus." You get a fair statement of those Mysteries in the Fathers of the early Church. It is stated that there were private teachings given by Jesus to His own disciples and apostles, that they were handed down by word of mouth and so preserved in the Church; and Origen, quite rightly, laid enormous stress on these.

You ought all to read those writings; there is one phrase of his which is very interesting, that the "Church has medicine for the sick"; "They that are whole need not a physician, but they that are sick," was one of the sayings of the Christ. Sickness means sin; those who were sinful needed the Church. But you could not make a Church only out of those who were sick; the Church had medicine for them, that was not to be denied; but you could not have a Church only for the sick. He puts it quite plainly and straight. In addition to this you must have the Knowers; they are the pillars of the Church.

It is the disappearance of those Knowers from the various great religions which has led to the comparative—not the entire—lessening of the influence of ceremonies. The ceremonies still have great value, because they are made for some particular purpose; but they have lost the added power that comes through knowledge. Some of you may remember that Shri Shankaracharya lays great stress on that, when he deals with a mantram. The mantram sets up certain vibrations which depend upon the words; any Brahmana who utters those Sanskrit words with their proper pronounciation and the proper sound of the mantram accomplishes some result, he says. But if the man has knowledge, the result is very much increased.

Every ceremony, rightly performed, has a value; it draws around it a number of Devas. A ceremony wrongly performed, and also without knowledge, has no value at all. It is just as though you had a mosaic with the pieces all loose and thrown down in a heap, instead of in their intended orderly arrangement; it would not have much value as a mosaic. Similarly, some ceremonies which are now performed at a certain religious shrine are useless, because the priests are ignorant. I heard them reciting mantrams there, and reciting them in bad Sanskrit. It was absolutely useless; the only value of the ceremony was that given by the worshipers themselves, the good though ignorant people who loved the one who had passed on, and were sending him waves of love. But so far as the ceremony went, it conveyed absolutely nothing, because the priests had neither knowledge nor accuracy.

Yet the character of the man who performs a ceremony does not matter so much. You might have a Brahmana of an exceedingly bad moral character, but if he were a good Sanskrit scholar and pronounced all his mantrams correctly, and if he made the gestures accurately, and performed the entire ceremony right, then that ceremony would have its effect on the astral plane, in Kama-loka. The fact that he was a man of bad morals would not influence that.

That shocks some people very much, because they are ignorant; but let us apply it outside religion, where prejudice and bias always come in. Supposing that a chemist were performing a chemical experiment, which was to produce a certain compound. If he put his substances together badly, he would not get his compound; he would get some sort of thing which might be either dangerous or useless, but he would not get his compound, because he did not follow out the laws of chemical combination. You say, that is quite right; naturally he did not get it. But suppose he is a man of very bad character, that he beats his wife, cheats his tradespeople, and so on. That will not make any difference in the production of the compound, if he obeys the laws of chemical combination. Those laws will not change because he is a bad man morally. Physical laws are not influenced by that consideration; if they were, we should never know where we were. How troublesome it would be if a chemical explosive, say, would go off properly for the good man, but would not explode for the bad man!

If you would apply that thought to morality, when you deal with Occult Science, you would be more reasonable in your demands than some of you are. I have known a good Roman Catholic to feel shocked because he was told, quite properly, that a bad priest does not injure the Sacrament. It would not be according to the realm of law if it did. His badness will cause bad magnetism, which he spreads through the church, but it does not alter anything that comes within his duty as a priest, if he performs it right, for exactly the same reason that the chemical compound follows the law of chemical combinations although the man who makes it may have murdered his mother the night before.

That is what you want to realize with regard to the study of Nature's laws. Obedience to the laws of Nature in one department does work out, no matter what the individual's relation may be to other laws of Nature. Suppose a man is a drunkard; then his eyesight may be bad and his fingers will not be trustworthy, and physical results will be brought about which will interfere with his experiments. But that is not caused by his moral vice, but by the fact that his physical body is affected by it, so that he cannot properly obey the physical laws which are necessary to produce the desired result.

It is vital for the understanding of Occultism that you should think clearly and accurately; otherwise you become very much confused. That is why Occultism is so dangerous to some; nearly everybody is a loose thinker, as you will, perhaps, remember if you contrast your present mental powers with what they were before you became trained Theosophists. Everyone who allows his mind to remain uncontrolled is barred from becoming a true Occultist, and any knowledge of Occultism is likely to be dangerous and mischievous to him, because he misunderstands and his devotion is apt to lead him all wrong. The way you see that working out is where a supposed occult authority comes into conflict with a moral law. A false authority wishes to be followed, because he claims to be an authority. But every "white" Occultist says: "Follow your conscience wherever it leads you; don't go against your conscience on the ground of what you think is occult obedience; that is not occult obedience." Hence any command against your conscience is a command to be disobeyed, no matter who gives it. And that is the only safety in Occultism; you must follow your conscience, and you must follow your judgment. Improve them as much as you can. But follow them.

CHAPTER VIII

SOME PHASES OF THE HIGHER CONSCIOUSNESS

In one of the earliest explanations given to us concerning man's evolution from life to life, the idea was suggested that karma is the guiding power, and trishna (thirst) is the force or energy which produces the new group out of the old skandhas for any given life. There is a certain divine law in Nature, this sequence that we call causation, or karma. That is, in the nature of things, drawn from Ishvara Himself; a certain definite sequence laid down, which we call cause and effect. According to that, events must work out. When a fragment of Ishvara, a Monad, comes out into Space and Time, then succession sets in; in Brahman everything exists simultaneously, but when drawn out under time conditions, the simultaneity becomes succession.

In that idea you have what we may call the fundamental definition of karma. It is the presentation under conditions of Time and Space of that which exists simultaneously without Time and without the extension which is the great characteristic of Space. That is what is called "the eternal Now." This is the root idea of what karma is: an eternal relationship, manifesting itself under conditions of Space and Time in any particular world. That is the guiding power in evolution; that is the only way in which things can happen here.

But what is it that brings us, as sentient beings, into this definite succession, this sequence of cause and effect? "Trishna" is the answer which we were given; the thirst or desire for sentient life. That is more clearly recognized if you study in your own nature the desires which rise up to experience certain things; that is what is very admirably called "the thirst." It is a natural uprising within the nature, equivalent to those physical cravings which you have, of hunger and thirst, for instance; the longing to feel, to experience, to realize your own existence by coming into contact with things which are outside your own particular sheaths.

If you think it over quietly you will easily recognize that in the state of things in which there is no experience of outside contact (remember that "outside" here does not mean in the physical world, but in all worlds), where there is no experience but the dwelling in that fragment which is yourself, then there is nothing which we call consciousness. There may be an intense internal life; but that which we know as consciousness (which is the distinction between one self and another) cannot exist. That can only come into existence for any special self when that self comes into touch with other selves. Hence it is said that the previous condition is one of unconsciousness. It is perfectly true that to the ordinary reader and thinker, whether in East or West (but very much more strongly in the West), that implies a state in which you may say there is an absence of life, because our experience of consciousness is all made up of these contacts. We have no experience outside of that.

When a man, by having practiced yoga for a long time, reaches a condition of things in which the sense of contact outside himself has disappeared, even then you must remember that he has gained that individuality or separation which consists in the memory of previous contacts; and in that he differs, say, from a fragment of Ishvara which has never come out into this kinetic condition, but has always been in a state of latency. In a sense, that is one of the enormous differences caused by passing through the experiences in matter. You never get rid of your memories of these; and when I use the word "memory" I am using it in a special sense; not that of the memory of events, but the change in yourself that has been brought about by going through the events, making a much fuller and richer content of consciousness than could be had without it. There are many other things as well, but that is one fundamental thing.

The man who has been practicing yoga for a very long time and has touched, say, the nirvanic consciousness, is not, while he is living alone in that state, conscious of external impacts; he is conscious only of unity, but he realizes an intensity of bliss, which is quite outside the ordinary meaning of what people call unconsciousness. And that is the point that I wish you to remember. It is the old difficulty that our words can express only the experiences through which the people have passed among whom the words have grown up. That which is beyond the words is by no means beyond the consciousness; but you cannot put it into any form which conveys a clear idea of it down here—it must be experienced. That is why I have laid stress upon the fact that you cannot convey the sense of a stage of consciousness to anyone who has not experienced that stage of consciousness. It must be an individual experience, and until the man has experienced it, there are no outer words that will convey to him what it really means. You may indicate it by analogy and picture and allegory, but you cannot really make it understood. He must experience it.

This is literally the same as the incapacity to convey to the lower animals a realization of what we are doing when we are thinking. There is no way in which you can convey to a dog (however much you may love him and however much he may sympathize with you) what to you is the reading of a book and thinking over what you read. He must inevitably think (if he thinks of it at all from his point of view) what a fool you are to sit there with a thing like that to look at, when you might be running about and enjoying yourself in the way that he would do. If you could look at the consciousness of a dog when he is waiting for his master to take a walk with him, you would find that that consciousness is not complimentary; it would be the reverse. We, who know both conditions, know that the dog is making a mistake and that we are enjoying a much higher type of consciousness than he knows in running about. But we cannot explain it to him. There is nothing that we can do to make that dog realize that the running around looking for a bone is a form of delight very much lower than we experience in reading a poem or looking at a picture.

While it may not seem complimentary to us in our present state, I cannot think of any better way of expressing the idea that you cannot convey these higher conditions to anyone who has not experienced them. And it is, perhaps, the experience of that on the lower planes that makes some of us realize that there are conditions of consciousness far beyond our reach, which are just as much out of our power to apprehend as our state is beyond that of a dog. We are bound to realize that, because we have experienced it in a lower phase. We cannot convey downward the experience of our own state, and we know that the Masters cannot convey to us the experiences of Their consciousness. That is why They cannot explain or make us feel that which is Their real life; for just as to us the mental and emotional life is enormously more vivid than the physical, so Their conditions of consciousness are enormously more vivid than ours; and the pictures that They have used of Their physical consciousness being like going into the dark, of the difference between one plane and another being like that of birth, death and so on, these are all similes to help us to realize it.

Hence, what to Them is the absurdity of the western idea in thinking that Nirvana is what the westerner calls unconsciousness? It is a condition of intense and supreme consciousness, far more vivid and far more blissful, far more superior in every way to what we call consciousness, than our consciousness is superior to the dog's. When that is recognized, the whole atmosphere of the universe changes to you. You are able to realize that you must not make a judgment on the conditions of consciousness of which you have no knowledge. There is no good trying to explain them or to define them.

You may remember that on one occasion the Lord Buddha, in an attempt to define it, said: "Nirvana *is*." It is a condition of existence; and in a Chinese version of one of His books of sayings, you find that worked out in a number of different expressions. One of them is: "The created and the perishable only exist because the uncreated and the imperishable exist." The real life is that which is beyond us. What we call "life" is only a derivative from that higher condition.

Anyone who has passed even into the astral consciousness (still more if he has passed into the mental) will realize that the whole ascending scale is a throwing off of limitations, and not a loss. We think of it as a loss, because to us it is unconsciousness; we learn by our lower experience that what seems unconsciousness to the one who has not experienced it, is an expansion of consciousness to the one who has experienced it. What we argue by analogy from that is the recognition of the fact that these higher states are fuller of life and joy and knowledge (if one may use that inappropriate word) than the most blissful and active are down here. That is really all that we need to grasp as what we may call the stimulus, the reason why we should try to climb. And it is necessary to have some such conception, however vague, because the passing to a higher condition of consciousness is always preceded by what seems like an extinction of consciousness. That is, we lose what we have; we lose all the distinctions and the differences and the limitations which are our consciousness. Those go, and we are obliged to have the courage to let all of them go, and we seem to be sinking into a condition of practical annihilation.

That is the great act of faith, to let it all go. It lies at the bottom of the words of the Christ: "He that loseth his life shall find it unto life eternal." That is what all the great Teachers tell us, and by our confidence in Them we are able to throw ourselves off what seems to us a rock of certainty into what seems to be the whirlpool of uncertainty that awaits us. When we do so, we find that it is not a whirlpool at all, but a greater life. We have behind us a certain amount of experience which grows fuller and fuller as we go on and on. But at every stage there is what the Christian Mystics have called "entering into the cloud"; and that is what is meant in that phrase of Patanjali's referring to this cloud. I once got an Indian friend of mine, who was a very fine scholar, to go around among the pandits of Benares to try to get them to explain this word in Patanjali, because we noticed that in the commentaries on Patanjali it was never explained. They gave what they called explanations, but they did not carry us any further.

To anyone who has so practiced meditation as to be able to pass on to another plane, that word becomes perfectly clear. It is the condition in which you are when you have lost the consciousness of one plane and have not yet gained that of the other. Everything below, that has been your life and consciousness, has gone. You are "in a cloud"; the phrase is most expressive. If you called it a London fog, you would perhaps have a more definite idea than the word "cloud" would convey to those who are familiar only with the light mists which you have here in India. Then you pass through it, and life on the other plane begins to express itself, at first in very vague forms, in the kind of way that you see buildings come through a mist as it begins to clear away. You get a glimpse of their outline, and they gradually become clear as the mist melts.

So with the realization of the higher planes. And that is why I have said to you that the word "knowledge" is out of place; you want to use the word "realization." That is what underlies that curious phrase in one of the Upanishats: "He who says, 'I know,' he knows not." Because the man who has achieved does not say, "I know"; he simply uses the phrase, "I am"—a realization quite different from knowing, or knowledge. You *know* that which is outside you; you *realize* that which you are. And so it ought always to be called the "realization," not the "knowledge." It is "knowledge" while you are knowing or not knowing; it is only when you have become God, when you can really say, " I am," that you have reached the condition which all the Rishis have described as the realization of God; and that, of course, cannot be taught by anybody.

Before you come to that, in all the lower stages, you have this "thirst" aroused in you, this "trishna," or "tanha," the desire implanted in your nature to feel and to know. And until the realization of Brahman is reached, that must always be; there is always something more, and when you have assimilated everything that you have, and when it has all become part of you, then trishna aagin arises and drives you out to seek new experiences.

It is, as I said, the same as hunger or thirst. There is need for liquid in the body, which expresses itself as thirst; a craving, a natural craving, showing a want. At first, it is a thirst for external experiences, and that is the sense in which the word "trishna" is used. There is a keener thirst, the want of the Spirit for Brahman. That has been expressed in exactly the same phrase in the Hebrew Scripture: "My soul is athirst for God; yea, even for the living God." There is no other word I know to express it so well. That is the thirst, the desire, of the part to find the whole to which it belongs. It is a very material way to put it; but if you could think of the part as coming forth, but never losing the link with the whole, never really going out of it; think of it as though it were a going outward which leaves behind part of itself which makes this connecting link—then there will always be a certain retractive force in it, trying to bring it back. There is no satisfaction outside divinity for the Spirit which is divine, and so long as he does not realize that full divinity, so long a sense of dissatisfaction remains. He wants his own, as it were; to be in the condition of all-knowledge and all-realization.

That is the root of trishna; dissatisfaction and desire to search, and that is, of course, what brings a person out of Devachan. He is hungry; he wants more experience down here. Similarly it will bring you out of any other condition where experience is needed, in order that the end may be reached. You see it in a curious form in what is called the natural law that water rises to the level of its source. There are mechanical explanations for that; there are always mechanical explanations whenever there is a phenomenon connected with matter, because you cannot have a movement of consciousness without a corresponding movement in matter. But the cause lies in the consciousness, not in the mechanism. That is the great blunder that the materialists have always made. When they find a mechanical change, they think they have found out everything. They do not realize that side by side with the mechanical is the change in consciousness which is answered by this mechanical rearrangement of the particles of matter. In that rearrangement, or the infinite number of rearrangements, there lie the things that science is able to discover by observation. And each one will satisfy the student until he begins to ask the question which it is said science cannot answer—Why? Why should this mechanical arrangement come about?

Take what plane of consciousness you will, there is some change of mood bringing about rearrangement of matter. And that thirst for the new experiences builds up the new being out of the old skandhas. There are all these tendencies which have left traces behind in the permanent atom, latent powers of vibration; but also there are a large number of atoms which have been in connection with that permanent atom in the past and have preserved a certain affinity with it. If rebirth is very quick, these are gathered together very much more freely, so that a quick rebirth means that you bring over a very easy regaining of the past consciousness. You have a great deal of your old material with you. If a long interval has elapsed, all these particles which were once yours have been entering into many other bodies, mixing up generally, and they are not so easily recoverable. You can only attract those which have something in common with your own permanent atom—some link. Those, which are literally innumerable and spread through the various planes, will gather round you, aggregate round the permanent atom, and form a new body.

You must remember that every semi-organized body with which the ego comes back to the three lower planes, has to be used for the gathering of new experience.

You know how much stress has been laid, especially by my brother, Mr. Leadbeater, on the result of the influences which surround a young child, even from before birth onward. Now that has puzzled some of our students because, while they accept what they call karma, they do not understand the laws under which new bodies are formed. The ego brings with him certain possibilities for moods of consciousness, which we call faculties. He brings with him, also, the mental, astral, and etheric matter roughly formed during the antenatal period, but only roughly formed; what you might almost call aggregations which had not yet been properly linked up.

As to the way in which this process proceeds, you can get a very good analogy in those peculiar cells in the brain which have been examined very closely of late years. There are somewhat larger cells in the brain cortex which do not subdivide as normal cells subdivide. You know how the growth of the body consists in a subdivision of cells already existing, a subdivision continually repeated, so that each of a group of similar cells subdivides; and that process goes on and on until you have a great mass of similar cells. That differentiation of cells begins by the action of cells within themselves and on each other; some change from the inside and some from the outside, according to differences of pressure, chemical change, and so on, in the antenatal period, until gradually you get the various tissues started out of these cells by external and internal causes, and the various organs build up out of the tissues which ultimately form the human body.

But there is a certain small set of cells which do not go through this process, but which work their way up to the upper part of the embryo; those do not subdivide, and when the child is born they are still separate and remain separate for a considerable period in the postnatal life. But changes go on within the cells, and they send out branches. These branches, after a time, meet. They come into contact, and the intervening dividing walls of the two branches are absorbed so that they are completely intercommunicating, and you have, so to speak, a channel—an intercommunicating channel. This process goes on and on for some seven years, until a fair network is formed, becoming more and more complicated later on.

That is where you find the physical reason for the seven years that are so much emphasized in connection with the coming down of the ego to take possession. Physiologists and psychologists (the two sciences run together very much during the early years) point out that until this complex network is made by the interlacing and intercommunicating of all these miniature roots, the child cannot reason to any great extent, and he ought not to be made to reason to any great extent; not that he should not see simple causes and their consequences, but he should not be given any mental process of complicated reasoning which might put upon him too great a strain. They therefore tell you, what the Occultist has always said, that the earlier years of life should be given to observation, rather than to reasoning. Get the child to observe as much as he can, and to acquire the power of observation. The senses are then very, very keen, keener than they are later in life. Utilize the early days for observation of facts, and let them be collected in the child's brain; but do not try to force him into any complicated process of reasoning. Let the life in the child, or, as we should say, the ego overbrooding the child, not receive impulses to anything that may not help this developing of the soul.

When this complex has been made out of the union of these separated cells, you have the part of the brain in which the reasoning process takes place; and these intercommunicating groups become finer, more numerous, more perfectly communicating as the child grows into the youth, the youth into the man, and the man grows mature. And the power of reasoning is growing all that time, scientists would tell us. What we say is that the power of reasoning in the ego is becoming more manifest as time goes on and it has a physical mechanism through which it can show itself in this outer physical world. Now while that is the case with the brain, there is a constant process of co-ordination going on also in the physical body, especially in the nervous system. In the lower mind the ray of the ego which is playing upon the mental body, as it were, from above and around, which develops the whole, is exercising on the individual child a pressure something like that which in the earlier part of the Race was exercised on the animal-man before the connection with the ego was made.

The individual and the race run along parallel lines. When the brain is ready, the ego comes more closely into touch and permeates it; that is, the causal body becomes linked up very much more with the mental body and then with the astral and the physical, and the whole becomes a single mechanism intercommunicating in all its parts. During the whole of this process the external impacts are enormously important in their play upon the consciousness. That consciousness, bringing with it the past skandhas, gathers round him again. It becomes, then, enormously important to help this growing life to choose the best possible materials to build into itself, and the influences which should be brought to bear upon it through the consciousness are those which ought to repel the less useful particles which would otherwise aid the lower types of consciousness in the ego to show themselves. Those should be starvel out by not giving them the material, mental, astral, and physical, which would enable them to manifest and to develop.

On the other hand one should try to stimulate all those faculties which are on the upward arc, by supplying any amount of good thought, good feeling, good physical conditions, so that everything that the young child comes into touch with on all these lower planes may be of the best. That ought to be the effort of the parent and also of the teacher.

It is obvious that with the ignorance nowadays prevalent, both in teachers and parents, all of this works out in a very haphazard fashion. It might all be co-ordinated to the best good of the child by proper knowledge, and that will be the case more and more as the races evolve. It was done to a great extent by the Rishis themselves in the past, when They were living among the people who were in what you might call the baby stage. They helped very much in all this arrangement of the influences around the children and so quickened their evolution.

Later the people were left to themselves to learn, and evolution for a time almost looks as if it were going back; it is not really doing so, but outward evolution for the time is not great. Then comes the period when, having developed large numbers of people to a higher stage, evolution becomes more rapid. So, during the Sixth and Seventh Races the rate of evolution will be great, compared with what it has been in the earlier stages, by the co-operation of human beings, highly evolved, who quicken the evolution of the lower racial types.

All that, as we have so often pointed out, will come back to us on a higher spiral. Meanwhile those who understand this can help very much in the evolution of the child, even though it is perfectly true that the nature of the ego is stronger than any outward circumstances you can bring to bear upon him in the way of education, and so on. The old phrase that "nature is stronger than nurture," which was temporarily reversed in the earlier stage of scientific progress, should be borne in mind. But nurture is of enormous importance, because it can starve out the bad germs and vivify the good ones. Artificial cultivation in that way quickens evolution to an extraordinary extent.

If you will remember that all through, you will be able to solve the questions that are often asked in connection with education. The child is a life that re-acts; it is not a mere thing that, as Robert Owen and others thought, could be created by its surroundings. That was the mistake upon which all the old socialistic colonies broke up; they still had human beings in them, and their idealistic schemes did not work. Now with an understanding of the two factors, very much can be done, if people live together who realize these things more fully. And we shall have that in the colonies which will form the beginnings of the Sixth Root Race; all these outside influences will be brought to bear, and the best possible conditions provided to evolve swiftly the beginnings of the Race. That is always done when a Race is beginning, and it is done to a very much more limited extent when a sub-race is beginning. Special care is taken to start it along the new line.

That is the reason why Theosophy should take the lead in education at the present time, at a time of transition like this. There is a certain amount of knowledge among Theosophists that enables them to judge of the value of the conditions with which the young should be surrounded, that enables them to see whether they are faulty, and enables them to suggest better methods.

It is because of that knowledge that Theosophists should take the lead in the great educational reforms which are now showing themselves as coming in, over the entire civilized world. You may notice that even in the stress of the struggle in England, there is a decided educational movement to prepare along better lines for that which will come after the War. The War itself has acted as a stimulus to a better line of education. In England there is much more opportunity for testing improved educational methods than there is here, for reasons which are well known to you. But even here in India we are doing the best we can, in the face of tremendous difficulties, to improve the educational system. Such is our duty as regards educational matters. How to do it will tax our very best qualities of intelligence and judgment. To go headlong into a scheme without careful consideration would be failure. Where you have to deal with physical matter and people encased in physical matter, you cannot change things as quickly as you can change them on the astral or the mental planes. Physical matter is not as plastic; it will break if overstrained. So we must use our best thought, our best powers of judgment, and exercise patience.

But we must seize every opportunity, and it is the seizing of opportunity which is the greatest deficiency in the character of everybody. More and more dealing, as I am dealing now, with occult knowledge in physical things, I find this difficulty in connection with some of the people with whom I am working. It is not a want of earnestness in them; it is not a want of goodwill; it is not a want of ordinary intelligence at all—there is plenty of all that. But it is a want of that particular alert faculty of the mind which, when an opportunity presents itself, seizes it at once and takes advantage of it.

There is very little of that faculty among us. You have to persuade people who are going along a particular path that they should change their way of going. To change the way in which they are accustomed to go means a very large amount of strength and courage, which few people possess. Therefore I do want all of you to try to develop that peculiar faculty which means the seizing of an opportunity and the holding it. You know it is the faculty which is developed among boys by the playing of their games. The difference between a good player and a bad player is that the former sees the moment when there is an opportunity, and he rushes forward and grasps it and wins. That is the kind of faculty you want in the important matters of life.

You want to grasp an opportunity when it is just passing through the air, as it were, and catch it and hold it; that means success. All around us opportunities float, and the great difference between people is not so much the difference of opportunity (as many of our Radical friends say), as the power to grasp an opportunity when it comes your way. There are a few people of enormously strong will who create opportunities, to whom the opportunity does not come, but who, meaning to be something or other, make an opportunity for themselves and succeed. Charles Bradlaugh was a man of this type. But there are others round whom opportunities, so to speak, are always floating—even knocking up against them.

But they do not see them or catch hold of them or do anything.

Now try to make all of your minds a little bit more alert in the sense that a good player of a game is always on the look-out and alert and always watching. That is what is meant in that phrase "seeing His slightest signal." It is the attitude towards the Master in which one is always trying to feel as He is feeling, and to act the moment one catches His thought. It means a great mental alertness and vigor.

It is the strained attitude of attention, exactly as you might be in if you were intently listening for a carriage coming from a distance. You are listening; something is approaching, and your ear is strained to catch the very first sound. You are in the very reverse of the condition of being indifferent and careless, so that if the sound came you would not notice it. The very first vibration of that sound would reach the ear that was tuned to hear it. It is that same idea that you want in the mental attitude. If you would only do that habitually, you would all be grasping opportunities and we should soon have things within our reach.

Another point in connection with the early development of the child is that of the conditions deliberately brought to bear on him. Some of the religions have tried to meet that. The Hindus had various ceremonies by which they surrounded with pure influences both the mother and the child before birth and after birth. The whole object of those was to create the special conditions which warded off the lower influences, and which, by that external help, also brought in the higher influences. That was devised by wise men, who understood these methods. They were accepted in those earlier stages by people who did what they were told, and so, by obeying, they gained the advantage of a knowledge of occult laws which they did not themselves possess. Now we are again working up to that by gaining knowledge of the law in a different way. Those ceremonies were very valuable; they had a certain effect on the developing infant, and they helped the child to have a better body, physically, astrally and mentally, than it would otherwise have had. It seems unfortunate that a large number of people, who ought to know better, have dropped these methods because they do not understand them. They are in a stage of evolution, an intermediate stage, when they have neither the teachableness of the child nor the knowledge of the grown-up man.

CHAPTER IX

MAN, HIS OWN RECORDING ANGEL

In explanations of karma it is frequently pointed out that each man, good, bad, or indifferent, records his character and his future by himself, through his thoughts, his emotions, and his actions. I shall give you a simile which may make this clearer. You know the way in which the scientific man records movements by curves which are drawn by a pencil attached to a lever, which in its turn is attached to the thing which is to be recorded—say the movement of the heart. The doctor puts over the heart a little instrument which is connected with a lever and a pencil. Against the point of the pencil there is a revolving axis covered over with paper. As that revolves, the pencil draws curves which exactly record the beating of the heart. If it beats more quickly, that is shown; if it beats more slowly, or more weakly, that is shown. Thus, that which is traced on this revolving roll of paper represents graphically the movements of that to which it is attached. In this case, by attaching the instrument over the heart or pulse, a doctor is able to see how that inner organ is working.

This principle is continually being used. It was in this way that Dr. Bose of Calcutta recorded the effect of various stimuli on minerals, vegetables, and animals, and showed how exceedingly similar they were; how plant and animal responded to the same stimulus. He had the movements recorded by the pencil on the revolving roll of paper. It is very interesting to watch it and see the life-movement record itself.

For our purpose it is enough to take the general idea, and to think of this record as being traced by the man himself through an apparatus that, for the moment, we may call karma. The man himself records all these causes that he sets going, and they work out in the future. In this way he is his own recording angel; it is not some outside power that makes the record for him, and then, on that making of another, that his destiny is created. It is the man who creates it for himself.

Let us for a moment look at this from the rather materialistic point of view of the bodies that are used by the personality—the physical, the astral, and the mental bodies. In these the consciousness of the ego is working. But these bodies perish; they are scattered back into the matter of the plane from which they were originally drawn. The physical body scatters its particles on the physical plane and they go back into the general reservoir of physical matter, with the impress upon them which the man has left, stronger or weaker according to the amount of consciousness which the ego had put down to vivify them during the time for which he had used them.

It is as well not to lose sight of the fact that this matter of the plane is being constantly modified by the egos who are working on that plane. They are impressing with their own characteristics all the particles which they use. Thus a particle of matter at the present time is extraordinarily different from a particle of matter as it was at the beginning of the manvantara. All these impressions which have been made upon it have increased its vibratory power.

There is nothing exactly corresponding to what you can call a "content" in the physical atom, but there is an enormously increased power of responding to certain vibrations. The power is latent; when something outside comes into contact with that atom, there is a response from the atom, and that response is according to the latent energy in it. It is in the same way that in ordinary physics you learn that when the force, or the energy (at one time everything was called force, at another time, energy; but now that has been turned round), becomes latent, it disappears; but it is there; it is not lost.

That is a good analogy to guide you in your thought of the mineral, vegetable, animal, and human sheaths. They all have this varying power of response in them, stored up out of their activities during the past. At death these particles are scattered; the form they made is gone. And that is true, in turn, of the astral and the mental bodies. Hence the Buddhist is perfectly right when he says that man (by which he is indicating these lower sheaths and the connections between them) does not continue, and when he quotes a phrase of the Lord Buddha: "There is in man no abiding principle; only the learned disciple who acquires wisdom knows what he is saying when he says 'I am'." We shall refer to that again in a few moments.

What does persist is the essential life of the ego; that remains through the cycle of reincarnations.

But you may say that that is not a permanent continuation, because that also, in its turn, gets drawn up through Buddhi into Atma, and so into the Monad, where you come to the really permanent. Sometimes in dealing with this I have asked people to remember that when they are speaking of the "I" they are going back to the Monad, if they knew what they really meant. It is in the Monad himself, the fragment of the Eternal, that man's eternity resides. Everything else is put out by that and drawn back by that; but the Monad himself is the "I."

That of course is not realized by people who know nothing about Monads; and others do not quite realize that the Atma proceeds from and is an extrusion of the Monad into our fivefold universe. So it is no wonder at all that this idea came into the minds of large numbers of the Buddhists, that there is no continuing personal ego, but only skandhas, the traces he has made. Taking them literally they are right; where they are wrong is that they imply that there is nothing continuing; that there is nothing beyond the personal ego. Normally, in talking with people about the higher constitution of man, you stop at the individual ego, because his separating sheath goes on through the whole cycle of births and deaths, which is quite enough for the ordinary person to grasp and think about. You only muddle him if you go much further.

The word "parent" has sometimes been used as indicating the relationship which the ego bears to the lower bodies of the personality, but it has to be taken with a word of explanation. (There is an interesting physical analogy which might be used here in the case of the permanent cell which passes on and on, only I must not go down that fascinating byway because of lack of time.) It is the ego (remember, also, what is behind the ego) which is the creator and fashioner of the latter, which is the personality; far more so, in truth, than any parent in the flesh.

Let us take the material properties or atributes of the personality—the lower bodies. The man is continually changing these. His physical body, for example, is perpetually changing. Modern Science has accepted this as a matter of course. You are not even exactly the same in your physical body when you go out of this room as you were when you came into it. Some of your physical particles have fallen upon your neighbors; some of theirs upon you. There is this constant interchange which is going on all the time; I have sent some of mine upon you; you, some of yours upon me.

That is what we may call the physical brotherhood of man. A man cannot live alone, even if he wants to do so. Even if he goes off into a jungle, he will get particles from the vegetables and the animals; he cannot isolate himeslf, when he lives in a world where all is related and interrelated. In dealing with the physical body I have often pointed out that there is a certain material and physical brotherhood which puts upon us certain duties and responsibilities and which brings upon us certain collective results for which in our separated selves we are not responsible, but for which we are responsible as part of the great collection of beings around us that we call Society.

Looking at it in that way, confining ourselves to the bodies, nobody would be foolish enough to say that what you have promised to do, say, before you came into this room, you are not bound to fullfil when you go out of it again, merely because physically you are a slightly different person. Technically you are different, but the *you* who promised is not these casual particles with which you are clothed. You pick those up and you throw them away again, and there is no more sense in calling those yourself than in calling your coat or your shawl or your shirt yourself. A man who has changed his shirt has not got rid of his liabilities if he is in debt, and his creditors would look at him very much askance if he said he had changed his shirt and therefore was not responsible.

It is that which is also the difference between you and your body. We identify ourselves with our bodies, but we do not identify ourselves so much with our clothes. We know we are always changing our clothes, but we do not know so much about our bodies. One is a visible and the other is an invisible change, but it is exactly the same thing really; and it is only as long as you are making that artificial identification of yourself with your body that you can possibly imagine that, because you are changing your body all the time, you are not therefore bound by all the liabilities which fall upon you through your thoughts, your feelings, and your actions.

I took an extreme case in the illustration of the change that occurs in the body in the interval between coming into this room and going out of it. But the whole of the body changes in a few years, and yet the man is responsible. That is the idea which has not only to be accepted (and of course we all accept it), but to be made a living part of one's thought, so that it covers and colors the whole of our thinking with regard to karma.

Carry on that thought to the next stage, the astral. Your physical skandhas, clearly, do not change *you*, the thinking, feeling, acting being, although all your actions on the physical plane are made through this changing body. Go on, then, to your astral body and you come to exactly the same thing: equally, all your sensations and emotions are not you; they are nothing more than temporary phenomena by which a portion of your consciousness is expressing itself in the astral world, as a portion is expressing itself in action in the physical world.

If you take it in the broad way, your will is expressing itself in the physical world through the physical body; your emotions, as we call them (the compact of sensations and thoughts), express themselves through the astral body; the element of thinking is expressing itself through the mental body. In the broad sense those are the three great aspects. I say in the "broad sense," because we have to remember that each of these is again divided into three, so that you get something of each of the other two in the one which is predominant. We must never forget that in the application of our ideas. Every particle of matter has in it the three gunas; one is predominant, and that is the one that gives the name to the aggregation; but, whether in the aggregation or in the single atom, all three are ever present, two latent, one patent.

You ought to keep that as a thought in the back of the mind, so that when I say the will expresses itself through the physical body as action, you will not exclude the other two; you will understand that I am naming the predominant attribute, that which impels to action, that which is called the massed-wish, the effective wish.

Carrying that idea to the astral body, you will understand that at the death of the astral body you are only shaking off another piece of clothing, another set of skandhas, those which have to do with sensations. Those scatter themselves again and become part of astral matter. But remember that they have gone through exactly the same process as the physical; they have become impressed by you; although the change is slower, it none the less goes on; there is nothing permanent there.

Go on to the next: you find the same thing happening with your mental body, and the make-up of that is continually changing under the impact of your thoughts. You are throwing out and you are drawing in; those particles which you throw out carry with them the impress of your past, while those which are drawn in you remold, and color and shape. The whole of this is going on all the time, and, when your life in Devachan is over, all of those go back again into the mental plane, into the general matter of the plane. Thus you observe that there is no difference in principle in all these changes which occur in the three bodies of the personality.

The tendencies which they produce, the tendencies which grow out of the impresses which you have made upon them, give rise to the skandhas, and to the powers that have become latent in them and that will be called out again in the future. Now the ordinary Buddhist says that the skandhas remain but the man has gone, because nothing can ever bring the whole of those particles together again. And it is true that the physical body has gone, the astral body has gone, and the mental also; what remains is the reincarnating ego and the permanent atoms attached to him, and the scattered particles.

You know, of course, the orthodox Christian conception that on the Resurrection Day we shall rise in our physical bodies. You may remember Voltaire's sarcastic remarks about this idea. He analyzed what happened; he said: The body dies, it decays, it becomes part of the soil, some of it grows into grass. Then a sheep eats the grass, the grass becomes part of the sheep, the sheep is killed for mutton, the mutton is eaten by a man. And so the original particles have passed into the body of another man. In the Resurrection, asks Voltaire, how are all these atoms to come together to clothe the original man? He points out that they have been used in the grass, in the sheep, and in the other man *ad infinitum*; then he leaves it for the Christian to explain. He says there is not enough matter for all these claimants to be clothed again. Then, if I remember aright, he makes a funny picture of the people quarrelling over a particle of matter; one man claims it for himself, another for himself, and so on—so that on the Resurrection morning there is a good deal of quarrelling among the people who are trying to get bodies with which to re-clothe themselves.

That was Voltaire's way, especially effective to a French audience, which is quick to see the absurdity of a thing. Nothing more fatally killed the idea of resurrection for the body than Voltaire's way of putting it. The people who believed in the resurrection were furious with him for what they called his "irreverence"—it was very irreverent for him to trace out the destiny of the body in that fashion and then make such a conglomeration of souls to struggle over its particles! But it was very effective to read, for you would never forget it. That was why Voltaire was so bitterly hated, and why to the present day he is often looked on as a sort of incarnation of jibes and sneers and sarcasms, which is a most false view of Voltaire. That was not the real Voltaire; he had all that brilliant wit in him which he levelled against the Church and the doctrines of his day. But you see much more of the real man when you remember how year after year he went on trying to get justice for the family of Calas, a Huguenot who had been murdered; for he went on and on until he got justice for them. That was the real Voltaire, who had a passionate sympathy for human suffering, and was willing to sacrifice everything for the sake of redeeming them. That side of him is not so well known. But that is a digression.

Now the question arises: What is there which may be called a skandha, which is picked up again when the man reincarnates? Clearly, it is not all these scattered fragments which have become part of the matter of the plane, and which, in addition to that, have been used by a large number of other people; for, supposing that you stay in Devachan for twelve or fifteen hundred years, a great many people have been using such parts of your physical, astral, and mental particles as they have come in contact with, and by congruity have picked up.

What remains is the permanent atom. But that conception was not given out in the early days; it was not even suggested in our earlier teachings, and only quite comparatively lately, during the last few years has this idea of the permanent atom come out. It was noticed as a brilliant nucleus in the causal body; that is what drew attention to it. Then some of us examined into it to see what it really was. In generally examining the things around, this was noticed and drawn attention to, and naturally at once the investigators wanted to know: What is this nucleus in the causal body and what does it mean?

It came to be connected at once in thought with the nucleus of a cell and the nucleus within it—matters which have been gone into so carefully in modern plant and animal physiology. It struck us at once as having something to do with the organization of the bodies, something to do with the building-up. So it was looked into very carefully, and the permanent atom came out of that investigation. The brilliant nucleus that was seen was the group of the different permanent atoms all together, all aggregated into a single body, as it were, with this exceedingly brilliant appearance which drew our attention it.

There lies what you may call the explanation of the skandhas. I think it is intended to be suggested in that phrase in one of our earliest writings: "The abstract mold, the privation of the future new being." You may remember how very fond H. P. B. was of that word "privation," and she used it very much to the annoyance of western people, because they never knew exactly what she meant by it. It was a word which had been used, I believe, in Greek philosophy, but her meaning was not quite the same as was attached to it by the Greeks. This annoyed the western scholars very much, and on account of their ignorance they ascribed it to what they called her "loose way" of thinking. They could not understand what she meant, and, to be quite frank *we* did not understand what she meant. We were fairly puzzled over this word "privation".

What she evidently did mean—which came out when we examined into the facts (and generally you did not learn until you found it out for yourself, and this made her so useful because she stimulated thought)—was that you did not retain anything which could be called material, anything which had a form. You had the abstract thing, which could generate an innumerable crowd of concrete things. That is what underlies her use of the word "privation," and whether the word itself is the best word that could be used or not, I do not know. But the fact that she intended to convey is quite clear.

It shows itself in the most startling fashion if you observe the change from an abstract idea, an arupa idea, clothing itself in the matter of the lower mental plane, the four lower sub-planes, if you watch the transition, as we have very often done. Take, for example, a triangle, which is so simple as a form. This abstract idea of a triangle is a reality to you on the arupa plane, difficult as it is to describe it down here. (Even trying to put it into words, one puts it into words wrongly.) It means a non-figure, which is yet a figure, which is circumscribed by three straight lines, the angles of which make two right angles. It does not mean any particular angle; it does not mean any particular line; but those two things must be present in order to make the abstract idea of a triangle.

Now that has an existence on the arupa sub-planes, and it has a reality there. With the sense of the causal body (if I may use the word "sense"), you do see it; you become conscious of it as external to yourself in what I am obliged to call a form. Because of our difficulties of language, that is fatally confused and muddled, because it is ony there that it is a *reality* to you.

Suppose that you grant such a triangle (if you can imagine granting it), and throw it into touch with the matter of the rupa sub-planes; it at once becomes an indefinite number of triangles, each of which has a definite form. You will have right-angled triangles, isosceles, and the other types, all coming into visible existence. If you choose to bring it down within your own causal body, you become a fountain of triangles which go off in all directions about you, as a jet of water, spurting up as a more or less coherent mass, and coming down as a fountain, separates into innumerable drops. There is no physical analogy which is more like it than that—drops thrown off in this descent, where there were no drops before.

You know that I have told you before that if you will be careful not to strain your physical brain, you can work up to this conception; in fact a few of our members have done it. I remind you of it again, because so many of you now here were not present when I mentioned it before. Don't try to do it too vigorously for the first time, because it tends to bring about a headache. It is better not to persist against that; a headache means that you are straining the nervous mechanism of the brain, which you must not do.

Take three triangles of different sizes and then of different forms; or perhaps it would be better to commence at first with three triangles of the same form—say isosceles. Think of the three separately at first and try to visualize them so as to get them clearly. Then try to bring those three together, as it were. Of course you will have a many-pointed figure, but do not mind that for the moment. Try to visualize that aggregate of three different triangles into a single triangle which has not lost the characteristics of the three. Then try to drop the outlines and keep the abstract thought of the triangle—the three straight lines and three angles that make up the total of two right angles. When you are just reaching that point (if you are successful) a certain change will take place in your consciousness.

It requires a number of weeks to accomplish it, because you can work for only a short time in the beginning. But when you have reached that point and are feeling a bit dazed in the effort to grasp it, your consciousness suddenly changes and becomes clear. That means that you have transferred the center of your consciousness from the mental body to the causal, and in the causal body you can see it; that is, you become conscious of it as a clear, distinct existence outside yourself. That is the intuition of the causal body, the intuition which recognizes the outer; whereas the intuition of Buddhi recognizes the the inner. You see things from *inside* in using your buddhic intuition; but you are realizing something *outside* yourself in the intellectual intuition.

That is one way of attaining this conception from where you are, from below upward. And you see at once why it is so difficult and so dangerous a thing to do unless you are very, very careful. It ought only to be done by a person who has practised meditation for some years, so that the tendency toward the causal body thinking has germinated; otherwise you can't get the result at all. But after some years of meditation you have established a certain tendency of the consciousness in the causal body to be affected by the consciousness in the mental body. It is the same consciousness, of course, but separated by sheaths; and when you have established that, you are able to undertake this by the process that I have been trying to describe.

In fact, the process really only becomes intelligible to you as you practice it. This is so often the case in the instructions for meditation. If you try to make out what they mean, you never get very much further, because you are keeping in the questioning stage of what is meant by it, which does not help you at all. Try to begin to do it and, as you do it, it clears itself, because the power is in you and you are calling it out. You call it out by doing it. In this case the "doing it" is the process of thinking, the definite activity of the plane upon which you are working.

There is no objection to any of you who are accustomed to meditation trying this, provided that you can remember to stop the moment you feel a little bit tired. If you are really doing it, you feel tired in a moment; then there is the temptation to go on further. Especially is that true of western people, who put their energy into meditation. You want energy in meditation, but it is the energy of the oriental rather than of the occidental type; that is, the energy which concentrates itself in the consciousness rather than in the sheaths of the consciousness. And, although that may not be clear to you, it is a fundamental difference.

I shall tell you the quaint expression which H. P. B. used on one occasion in making that clear to me. She asked me to will something simultaneously with herself. I began to do it in the most vigorous way, when suddenly she stopped and said: "My dear, you don't will with your blood vessels!" I had been willing so energetically, in my western way of doing it, that I had caused a great rush of blood to the head, the result of which was that my arteries were expanded almost to the point of breaking. Of course, she was watching and stopped it.

If you have any physical sensation, you are willing with your body and not with your consciousness. That is the thing to remember: that is the danger sign. If you feel tense (and you know how often, when you begin to meditate, your body gets tense) that does not help your meditation, but it does injure your body. When you are meditating, stop for a moment and feel how your body is. If you find it is very tense, stop and relax; otherwise you are straining it.

At first you can't help it, because the habit for

thousands of years has been to make the body follow the consciousness. If you think hard you begin to frown; you do it naturally. You fix your eyes when you are thinking intently; your eyes get tired. These physical accompaniments are the things that are tiring. You say that *you* are tired of thinking; no, *you* are not, but your *body* is, for you have made it follow your thought, which the poor thing cannot do beyond a certain point. If you try to make your body do it, it gets tired.

If you notice children, you will see that very strongly in them. The whole body works with the mind. Observe the child learning to write, and see the faces he makes; he shuts his teeth hard; he makes his mouth twist; he puts his head on one side—all in the attempt to write a single letter of the alphabet. It does not help him in the least, but the child cannot avoid it.

That is the tendency in all of us. We do not do it to that extent, but if you suddenly pause when you are thinking hard (if you have not trained yourself otherwise), you will find the same tendency in the body. As long as it does this, you cannot use the whole power of concentration of your mind, because you are wasting it in this physical exertion, and the whole body gets tired.

If you have got beyond that, then, when you begin this attempt at perceiving this peculiar kind of triangle, you will have for a moment a little sense of being dazed, then a burst of new consciousness, and then you will "see" this formless thing. It sounds absurd, but it is not. That is the process of climbing up to it. The reverse is the case when you come down; then you pull this formless triangle with you, and it shoots out into all the different kinds of triangles, into a kind of spray of triangles, as said.

When you have accomplished this, you will realize what is meant by the skandhas, and the privation of matter—these inherent qualities which persist after death, and which are the basic factors in determining what shall be the character of the bodies of the personality in the next earth-life.

CHAPTER X

DIVINE VERSUS HUMAN JUSTICE

In our consideration of karma there is a case which illustrates how justice is done by the divine law when man-made laws are so unjust. An illegitimate child has no social tie with his father; he has no civil rights, no name, he belongs to no one, he is nobody. While he is an infant there is a responsibility upon the mother, but none upon the father except where he can be proved, in which case he may be forced to contribute to the cost of maintaining the child. From its infancy the child is branded and suffers all his life long.

From the ordinary standpoint that is the greatest injustice, because the child is not responsible for what the father and mother did, so that he is suffering for a thing over which he had no control at all; he is born for the first time and he is born under a curse from which he can never escape all his life long. Clearly there you have a very serious injustice. That which would be said for the justification of it is that the individual is sacrificed to the State or Society. Marriage and legitimate descent being of value to Society, the person Society can get at is punished —the illegitimate child. On him falls the penalty, the idea being that unmarried people are very often prevented from having a child by the fear of having this penalty put upon the child. They are thus appealed to through the unborn child.

From the standpoint of karma, injustice is avoided by an individual being guided to that particular birth who has deserved it by his own past. He is born without all these civil rights, with that brand put upon him, through his own life in the past, because he has done some actions (we may not know what particular ones led up to it, without individual research) which make that the inevitable outcome.

That, of course, is where karma comes in. You cannot suffer for another person's fault; you suffer for your own. And so the divine law, through karma, justifies what would otherwise seem unjust.

Another question about which difficulty arises is how people are guided into or kept away from accidents. You cannot suppose that there was any particular arrangement, say, with regard to a person who was killed in a railway accident; you cannot suppose that everything was arranged beforehand in order that that particular person might be killed. But the real explanation is that that particular person is the one who is guided into the middle of the events; not that they are all arranged for him. It is he that is guided into a mass of circumstances which enable his own individual karma to be carried out; that is, his own deva takes him in hand and just guides him in that particular way.

Let me explain how it might happen in a town like London. Suppose a man is going to a train where there is to be an accident, but that it was not intended that he should go there and be killed. He would be stopped on the way, perhaps by a block in the road. If you look at it from the standpoint that that block is caused for the sake of that one man, then you get into a great many difficulties, because you have to imgaine that some hundreds of people are all specially influenced to drive to this particular spot in order that this particular man may be saved. But if you take the fact that there are always blocks in London caused by the crowding of the traffic, then it is an easy thing that his driver should be influenced to drive a way on which a block should stop him. In the working out of karma you have the assistance of a number of superphysical beings, the devas, who are continually concerned with the affairs of men, and who thus take advantage of such situations; and that is the way that the working of the law is adjusted.

Exactly the same principle rules in astrological predictions. People very often make fun of astrology because they say: "Do you suppose that all the planets are put in a particular position in order that So-and-So may be born at a particular moment?" The answer of course is that the planets come naturally into all these particular positions, and the birth of the child is regulated to suit the planets, not that the arrangement of the planets is regulated to suit the child.

Sometimes you will hear people say: "How can astrology and karma both be true?" They are two different ways of putting the same thing. If you can get that conception of the larger plan, in which at any given time a mass of different conditions are going on in different parts of the world or of a neighborhood, then you will see that all that a deva has to do is what, say, a mother might do with a child: take hold of the child's hand and lead it along a particular path, prevent it falling or let it fall, whichever she may think is best for the child at the moment. That is more the relative position of the two; the deva is in the position of the guardian.

That is the Christian idea of the guardian angel. The guardian angel is attached to the child from birth, looks after him, pushes him here and there so as to suit the particular lessons which he is to receive, and generally acts as an influence which guides him into or away from certain conditions and circumstances. All those, from the standpoint of the East, are karmic happenings, conditions taken advantage of in order that the individual karma may be worked out.

Again, there is the phrase from the Bible, that the Lord visits the sins of the fathers upon the children unto the third and fourth generation. That is quite literally true, for you can see it clearly in many cases; if, for example, the father is a drunkard, he transmits physically to the child and the grandchild a certain lack of nervous equilibrium, a certain tendency to nervous disturbance, and all the rest of it. That would be very cruel if it were the first birth of the afflicted child, and if it came upon the child without any previous reason in the child's own life.

But it becomes perfectly rational if the child in the past has been a drunkard; he may not have worked off all of that tendency in Kama-loka by the inevitable sufferings that come upon such a person after death. It is true of drunkenness and of any other abnormal physical passion, that the suffering from it after death is of a very terrible character; besides it is far more difficult to get rid of the tendency than if the person had the common sense to fight it during his physical life, when he has a great advantage, and when it is far easier to fight than it is after the physical body has been struck away by death.

Suppose you take such a case. I have known two or three of these, because I have come into contact with several drunkards whose past I looked up because I had to help the people. I mention especially that of a person who had been given very much to excess in drink. He was born into a family of drunkards and inherited their physical disabilities. Yet he had a horror of drink from the time he was a very little child. It made him sick, and if drink was put to his lips by his father or mother, he would push it away; he was disgusted with it.

But he used to dream of drinking, and in his dreams he still suffered from it. This disturbed him very much, because in his physical, waking life he was entirely against it and shrunk from it. He asked why this was. Of course I explained to him that in the first place the disgust came from his experience in Kama-loka after his last death. He had suffered so terribly there, from the craving for drink which could not be satisfied, that it had left impressed upon the permanent atom this horror; so that quite naturally he pushed it away when it came near him in his next birth. He was born with the disabilities from the drunken parents because he had made them for himself. He still felt the inclination to drink which he gratified in his dreams; that was the memory of his past impressed upon the astral body, so that when the control of the mind over the physical body was lessened during sleep, he yielded to the thought of drinking. It was quite obvious to tell him: "When you go to sleep determine to yourself that you will not take the drink when it comes before you in your astral life; decide to reject it then, and it will go." That is what he did, and it happened as I told him, and he finally cleared away that particular karma.

We must recognize definitely that the physical karma which we see in an individual is related to some past physical, mental, or moral karma which we may not see; that you cannot separate mental phenomena from material phenomena, and that there is no such thing in our world as an action of consciousness which is unconnected with some form of matter.

The materialists there are entirely right in that part of what they say. They say, you never find mind apart from matter; that is true, you do not. Matter may be subtle, but it is matter none the less. It is made up of atoms; those atoms are aggregated into molecules. Whenever you get a change of mood in consciousness, there is a change of relative arrangement in the particular kind of body or sheath in which that consciousness is working. So far as Science has ever been able to trace this correlation between mind and matter, it has been found to be invariable.

A difficulty at first arose when they began by hypnotic and mesmeric phenomena apparently to get hold of consciousness (as far as they could tell) apart from matter. That is to say (in the hypnotic trance of the deeper kind), when all the matter which they knew about was paralyzed and was not answering to stimuli, they still found mental activity. That was, perhaps, the first great blow which was struck at the whole materialistic hypothesis, because this was irreconcilable with it. In my own experience I may say that was the subject that first made me see that the materialistic hypothesis was insufficient. Not that it was not true as far as it went; it was true in its series of facts; but I saw that there were facts that it could not explain.

I do not know that there is any better way for a scientific man, who has gone through all the scientific facts and become a materialist, to get out of it, than by the study of hypnotism, mesmerism, and spiritualism. Any one of these will bring him face to face with mental and other phenomena which he cannot explain. That is the easiest way for him to advance, because he has the phenomena and he is not taken away from the region of experiment which is vital to the scientific man. It is no good telling him that he must leave the tools with which he is accustomed to work; he won't leave them. You have to reach him while he is using those tools.

I may feel a little strongly on that point because that is the road I myself came along. I studied Science in its most materialistic stage in the last century. It is very satisfactory as far as it goes, which is a thing which very many people hardly realize who have not studied it, and who have started with and held to the spiritual side.

Take for a moment the materialistic argument, as it was put and proved in those days when physiology first began to make its great impress on psychology. Before then the two sciences had been apart, separated. People had studied physiology; they had also studied psychology; but they never studied them together. Now the eastern view of psychology, as it is normally taught in the East, begins, so to speak, in the air. You don't know where you are. But western psychology begins on the ground, and you never get away from it.

Then began the study of psycho-physiology, and it is that which has led practically to the downfall of materialism in the scientific world as a complete theory of life. The old argument (I might just remind you of it in case you have never gone through it carefully) is based on the physical changes which are correlated with the gradual growth of consciousness from birth to death—a quite definite series. The newly born child is to all intents and purposes unconscious of the cause and place of pain; if a pin runs into him he screams, but so far as any mental phenomena are concerned, they are not there at first. As the child grows, consciousness begins to show itself, but in an exceedingly inchoate and senseless sort of way. As the growth of the child continues, consciousness becomes more and more definite, and it begins to make relations between things—which is the essence of thought. Then, as these go on, there are certain concurrent changes in the brain. Special cells in the brain (whose action I explained in a previous talk) send out their roots in various directions, and so the physical machinery of thought is produced. In the old, materialistic days the origin of thought was expressed in that famous sentence:

"The brain secretes thought as the liver secretes bile."

That was the position, and there was a great deal to uphold it when the growth of the brain was observed. The brains of people dying at different ages were examined; there was found a very clearly marked succession of changes. The brain of a man of great intelligence was found to be very different from the brain of a clown in its convolutions, their direction, quantity, and so on. Then they noticed that wherever there was a physical disturbance, there was also a thought disturbance. If a man gets drunk, his thought gets intoxicated at the same time, confused, bewildered, senseless. If his temperature goes up, his thought becomes delirious. If he is knocked on the head, his thought vanishes. Where does it go to? If the man is trepanned, his thought comes back. Gradually, as he gets old and passes into senile decay, the thought also becomes weak and feeble, and second childhood sets in.

If a portion of the brain is taken away, memory also goes; he can't remember; it is a case of amnesia. Take one remarkable instance of the moral effect of brain lesion, which is on record (there are a large number but I mention only one of them): the case of a young workman who was a very decent-living man, courteous in speech—nothing remarkable about him, but a very decent creature altogether. He was working at blasting with dynamite, when the charge exploded too soon. The iron rod with which he was working was thrown by the force of the explosion through the side of one eyeball, and it went through the front of the brain and out the other side. One thought that he would have been killed, but he was not. He recovered, but his whole moral character was changed. He became foul-minded, profligate, and after a little time he had no character at all; he became an absolutely disreputable, indecent creature.

It is no wonder that scientists marvelled at these phenomena. That is just a striking one that I take from Ferrier, who was a great brain specialist. Can you wonder that people said that a man's character depended upon his brain when, if a piece of iron went through it, his character changed? What stronger proof can you have that a man's moral qualities are the result of the configuration of his brain? It is a difficult question to answer unless you have Theosophy, which explains the whole thing. But when there was no proof from the scientific standpoint that a man survived death, when they found that during his life his changes in character, including his mental and moral character, depended upon the condition of the brain, one could not blame them (or any of us who studied these things) for coming to the conclusion that the thoughts and the brain were causally connected in the fullest possible way.

It was only when one commenced to study dream phenomena, and mesmeric and hypnotic phenomena (which, after all, are only the condition of consciousness in trance, which is a deeper form of sleep), that one began to see that while the scientific induction was true as far as it went, it did not go far enough. We did not have all the facts; it was a true induction on the facts we had. And there lies the weak point of inductive reasoning: it is so difficult to be sure that you have all the facts. If you have not all the facts, then, however perfect the induction, you may come to a wrong conclusion by virtue of the facts that are left out. If what is called your "universe of discourse" is complete, then your induction is sure. But suppose it is not: suppose there are a great many mental phenomena which, when you come to deal with them, do not come within the limits of those on which your result is founded; then of course it cannot stand; and that is what happened with us.

Dreams were the first to shake the position, because the measure of time and of space changes in dreams. At first the psychologists were inclined to think of this as without connection with matter, because it was out of connection with matter as they knew it. And if you have ever gone very carefully into mesmeric and hypnotic phenomena, you know how extraordinary the results are; how you can have a person either wholly senseless in deep trance, or you can paralyze parts of him and inhibit certain activities, when there is no outside sign that they are inhibited. You can make him blind to a particular person in a room, when he can see perfectly well everybody else there.

Extraordinary results were obtained in that way; and as they accumulated, we had to recast our theory. The question which finally arose was: Do you put them apart from matter because they are apart from the physical matter of the brain, or do you carry on your investigations further into matter, to see whether it manifests in other forms than the forms that you normally deal with in the laboratory? That is really the position that you finally come to. Of course, when you develop any form of clairvoyance, you begin to examine all kinds of matter, and to solve satisfactorily these perplexing questions.

Science has reached the point where it judges by results, and argues up to other kinds of matter by reasoning, not by experiment; and that is the extraordinary change which has come over the scientific world. Where they used to argue from experiment they now go beyond experiment and, finding results, they argue up from results to that which produced them; whereas they used to argue downwards from the things which they discovered to an explanation of new phenomena. It is an immense change in mental attitude; I have sometimes put it that they now take force for granted because of its results on matter, whereas they used to deal with matter only and try to discover in that something which caused the results.

Some now are going further; some now are beginning to realize that there may be possibilities of experiment by some inner evolution of man, by keener senses. That, I think, is being to some extent quickened among the more thoughtful of the scientific men of today by the observations that we made and called *Occult Chemistry*, several of which have been verified. If you can get even a few observations made years before Science has touched them, and then let Science come slowly up to them in its own way and discover them for itself, and then (metaphorically speaking) throw the book at their heads and say: "Well, here it is; it was discovered ten years ago," you make them think.

I don't say that you convince them in this way; I don't think that they ought to be convinced so easily. You want that they shall find a large number of corroborative data, which they will all finally see, and thus be convinced. But finding two or three in this way will make them wonder; it may make them more receptive. Frankly, I do not think they ought to be convinced by our occult investigations, because to their minds there might be other explanations.

Therefore, personally, I never feel any grudge against the slowness with which scientific men adopt what is really an unproved thing. Their scepticism is very healthy and much more likely in the long run to give a firm foundation on which they can build a proof which will convince the mass of the people. I don't see why we should want to hurry them and make them jump to conclusions.

All that the clairvoyant ought to hope to do is to act as a kind of signpost for investigation; not at all to resent the repulse, or the suggestion that his prior discovery is an accident, or a chance, or a coincidence. Let him take all that and say: "Well, let it be so." As you multiply those cases it will convince them; but you must be willing that they should multiply before scientists will be willing to accept them. There is also a certain kind of scientific pride which makes it annoying to them to find that something at which they have just arrived after much labor was discovered by clairvoyance some years ago.

It is a widespread human quality, that pride; one does not like another to come along and say: "Yes, I knew that years ago." One is apt to resent that. Yet if you feel sure of your own results you do not resent it. The only people who resent things are the people who have a little doubt; and because the repulse strengthens the doubt, they get very angry. That is the position of most religious people; at the bottom of their heart they have a little doubt—now is this true after all? They know they cannot prove some of the religious doctrines about which they are most emphatic, but they don't like to feel they can't prove them. They cling to their religion because of an intuition which they cannot understand, and they are quite right in doing so.

But they get terribly angry when suggestions are made which they see are reasonable; so they lose their temper. If they are in the majority they subject the offending individual to torture, because the one thing to do with him is to shut him up; no matter what happens to him, shut him up. You feel resentful only so long as you doubt. When you are sure, you can take the wiser attitude and say: "That is what I believe; you will find it to be true, but I don't care when you accept it; I know it is true." And you will not feel a bit resentful if they do not accept it, for you know that ultimately they will come to it.

One must say this of the European scientist: he is pre-eminently honest. I do not mean that he is not prejudiced; everybody is. Before he is willing to give way he wants more proof than it is quite reasonable that he should have. But that attitude is, after all, very advantageous in helping to establish the truths on such a basis that the mass of the people will accept them.

Science is gradually approaching an understanding of the fact that life underlies all forms of matter.

It does not yet see, as we do, that spirit and matter, consciousness and matter, are inseparable. That is why, of course, we have this particular Society, the Theosophical Society. It is an affirmation of that great truth that spirit and matter cannot exist apart, except in the Absolute, and there they are unified and not apart.

CHAPTER XI

NON-PHYSICAL BEINGS: I

In all religions there is mention made of non-physical beings. Some higher than men and some lower, for the worlds which are subtler in their matter than our own have their own inhabitants. Among these there are human beings, but also very many who are non-human, and who are evolving along lines other than our own.

In the Deva Kingdom, the Kingdom of the Shining Ones, there is a broad dividing line, the so-called "embodied" and "bodiless" Devas (the rupa and arupa, with form and without form). The Christian divides this same Kingdom into Angels of nine Orders, and the great hosts of fairies, gnomes, elves, brownies, sylphs, undines, etc. Modern materialism empties all the worlds but the physical, leaving us only men and animals as conscious beings, and making the physical a lonely globe, and a far duller one than in the elder days, when ripples of laughter of faun and nymph were heard in every glade, and all nature was alive in every part.

The "bodiless" Devas are so-called because they dwell in the subtle regions where matter is subdued to Spirit and takes shape at the Spirit's will, those regions which belong to the three aspects of Spirit—Intellect, Wisdom, Power; the embodied are among the inhabitants of the lower mental and the astral worlds. The "bodiless" Devas are connected with the guidance of the worlds, of races, of nations, while the "embodied" have to do with the shaping and guiding of the Kingdoms of Nature, and are in the astral world instinctive rather than intelligent. Mentality is little developed till we touch those "embodied" in the lower mental world.

Some in the higher class of Devas have been through our humanity. They are those who, having passed through the stage in which spirit and matter are in conflict or balance, have passed through the five great Initiations and have chosen to join the cosmic class of Arupa Devas, one of the seven Paths. You will remember that there are seven Paths which are open to the Jivanmukta after Liberation is attained. When the fifth great Initiation is passed, there are seven distinct lines of further evolution, any one of which may be selected. One of them is that which is usually called in the later Theosophical books the Deva Path. That does not belong exclusively to our world; it belongs to the whole solar system. We are not concerned for the moment with those who go up to it directly along a special line of seismic evolution from the beginning; that, you will remember, has been traced out, coming up through the fishes and birds and so on. This is only one stage in their evolution, and it goes on into other worlds.

That immense class of Arupa Devas may be joined by a human being after he has passed the fifth Initiation. He may, after he has reached that, go off into that cosmic class. Then his evolution becomes of a very different character, going round the different planetary chains of our system and so on. They rise, of course, to enormous heights of evolution, and it is from among those that the great future guardians of the various planets are found. I think it is in *The Inner Life* that Mr. Leadbeater mentioned that in touch with the Occult Hierarchy of our own globe there are certain great Beings whom he speaks of as Ambassadors—that is, Beings who come into touch with our world from other planets. Similarly there are others, who come from outside the solar system. Those are very, very lofty Beings, and they do not deal individually with people; they are not concerned with individuals. They are concerned with great cosmic processes. Those in touch with our world are the immediate agents for the carrying out of the law of Karma, especially as regards the changes in our world, the changes of land and sea, the changes brought about by earthquakes, by tidal waves, by all these great seismic causes. They are the immediate agents in them; in those particular changes they act under the orders, of course, of the Head of the Occult Hierarchy. It is He who has the Plan.

You remember that there is a Plan which affects the whole of our system under the Logos Himself. That Plan is divided up among the different chains. It is subdivided again, with so much to each chain, and then subdivided among the various globes. So far as this globe is concerned, that Plan is in the hands of the Head of the Occult Hierarchy. That Plan is referred to in *Man*, and it is stated there that the Head of our Race, the Lord Vaivasvata Manu, was shown the part of the Plan which affects His whole race. The entire evolution is sketched out. Each great Official has so much of it to superintend. It is as the plan of the architect of a building, and he has so many overseers; each overseer gets so much of the building, which he looks after, and it is his business to see that the workmen in connection with that part carry it out perfectly. Whatever grades of workmen he has below him, they are all responsible to him. And in that way, when each man has done his part, the whole of the building is perfectly co-ordinated.

There comes in the reason for that absolute unity of will which characterizes the Hierarchy, and also the perfect subordination of one grade to another. The whole arrangement of the world would fall into confusion if there were what down here is called the play of free will; that is, if you had anarchy instead of order, if all the various wills of human beings went off on their own account without any co-ordinating force. Now, so far as the wills of human beings are concerned, they are prevented from any serious disturbance of the whole Plan; but they do affect the individuals whose wills are thus expressed, and sometimes great confusion results from that which is sown here on the physical plane. Afterwards it is realized that all these individual wills are part of the larger Will, and that larger Will is seen as the whole, and the individual will is seen as part of it. That is indicated in the Church Collect: "Whose service is perfect freedom." The moment you have identified your will consciously and deliberately with the Will of the Higher, from that moment you have no sense of obligation or compulsion, but only a joyful cooperation with the Hierarchy. And it is at that co-operation that all those who desire to be disciples aim.

Now in these Devas that is of course perfectly developed, otherwise you could not have any order. It is developed in the whole Occult Hierarchy for the same reason; and when the Lord Vaivasvata Manu was shown His part of the Plan, He simply took it and He keeps it as a part of His book of directions, as it were. It is always by Him, and He guides Himself by that. Hence the perfect "order," as it is called, that you find in Nature.

Those who are lower down in the Deva Kingdom obey instinctively; that is, they have not yet developed that combative, challenging, questioning power which is essential to evolution. It is a stage of evolution and there is no harm in it; but it has to be placed within certain restrictions and limits, so that it shall not be allowed to disturb the whole; within those it plays about. These distinctly lower Devas move to a great extent automatically under this impulsion, of which they are not even conscious, and do not therefore trouble themselves about it; they do their work, feeling impelled in its direction.

The Devas who are beyond the fifth Initiation normally live in that which is called in Sanskrit the Jnanadeha, or the body of knowledge. The lowest part of that is an atom of the nirvanic plane, serving them as our physical body serves us.

The Spirit of the Earth, that obscure being, who has the earth for his body, that Planetary Spirit whose evolution goes on with the evolution of the physical world, is not of the highest order of Devas.

We know very little about him, and the matter has apparently not been investigated very far by any of us. He may be said to belong more to the Rupa Devas, because he has this earth for his body.

Let us consider the other inhabitants of the astral world, and pause for a moment on the "ghosts." In some of the earlier nomenclature there were the "two-principled" ghosts, beings, who are still working in the physical etheric double, with an admixture of lower astral matter which they envelop and largely paralyze. Those include one type of "shells"; that is, they go on living actively for a time after the man himself has left them behind.

Think for a moment of the normal thing that happens on the astral plane after death, when the astral body settles down into its various densities, the concentric shells that are so often spoken of. Now the ghost has one or two of these in connection with the etheric double. These are the beings who automaticcally repeat what had been the dominant thought during the period of their life upon earth. They originate no fresh thought; there is nothing to originate there, because the emotional and the mental bodies are not present. They are mere animated forms, vivified with what you may call a memory of the past life on earth, and repeating over and over again the more material actions and impulses that dominated them during their earth-life. Unless that domination had taken place, there would not have been this stage to any extent after death. The etheric double would disperse so rapidly, the lower shells would have broken away so quickly from not being vitalized, that there would have been a mere passing phase of no importance at all. The man goes on, and these remain behind, floating about and of no consequence.

These are the beings who very often frighten people who are to some extent psychic. That which is left of consciousness is mere habit of the lowest portion of the astral body, the worst part. It is the more antagonistic side of the human life; and one reason why you should not allow any thought of anger, annoyance, or anything of that kind to remain in the mind is that any such thought vitalizes this lower astral matter, and so you tend to prolong the stupid, senseless life of this wandering creature afterward, who may act as an annoyance to other people.

H. P. Blavatsky used to speak of them with a kind of mingled amusement and contempt; not an unkind contempt, but looking down upon them as silly things. She could not see why people should be afraid of them. I remember her saying once that one of those ghosts had come in and stood alongside her bed the night before, that he had only a face, and that there was no back to his head; she said: "I can't understand why people should be afraid of a creature like that."

It is the unknown that terrifies; for if you realized exactly what this creature was, you certainly would not be afraid. But if you only saw this kind of form floating up near you, without much consciousness of the fact that you were there and generally not inclined to be agreeable, but rather disagreeable, it would be natural to be frightened. You might not know that it was a sort of innocuous, senseless creature, and that just a mere whiff of your will would drive it away and send it elsewhere. Of course ignorant people cannot understand that, and so they very often get alarmed.

Those are one of the classes which are sometimes found in connection with the lowest type of spiritualistic medium. They always tend towards the earth atmosphere naturally, because they have the etheric double, which is physical, and they have only these lowest tendencies which draw them towards the place to which they really belong. Hence you have large numbers of these floating about, who will be attracted to people who have any ideas or notions or thoughts of a kind germane to themselves, and also to all places where there is a chance of getting into physical touch again.

It is there that lies one of the dangers to ignorant people of the lowest type of spiritualistic seance. A creature of this sort fastens himself on to a person who is a little mediumistic, who may happen to go to a seance, and he becomes very troublesome; he makes taps, rings bells, shakes beds, and does all sorts of stupid things, which are annoying and alarming to people who do not know that there is nothing to be alarmed at. They are sometimes a little troublesome to get rid of, because the person annoyed does not know he can get rid of them by the exercise of his will. He only becomes frightened, and any sense of fear gives them more power.

I imagine that under these might also be included those very remarkable survivors from the past of which Mr. O'Donnell has written so much, and which are rather alarming. He seems to have run across an exceedingly unpleasant type of this kind; possibly also of another type we shall come to in a moment.

They seem to be survivors of the earlier races who inhabited the earth, and who hang about a very limited area, of which the centre was the place of burial of those people. I don't know whether we have anything of the kind in India, but there are some of these huge burial mounds in Europe and many also in America. They are just mounds of earth, and they look like natural hills. When these are dug into, they are found to contain bones and other remnants of the very early inhabitants of the world, corresponding to the very primitive type of human beings known to geologists. It does appear as though some of these had managed to retain a certain amount of life, and they hang about these particular places and cannot go far from them—one of the marks of the etheric double being present.

In those animal-men only the crudest forms of passions would exist, using and vitalizing to the utmost the lowest forms of astral matter, and their attitude to a stranger would always be one of bitter hostility and desire to slay. Is it possible that such beings could exist through immense periods of time? I have not looked into the matter, so cannot speak positively, but it seems more likely that the men should long ago have passed onward, and that their forms should have been taken possession of by other entities of a malignant type, preserved and renewed. This is only a suggestion, on the supposition that Mr. O'Donnell is relating psychic experiences, and not merely clever and vivid stories woven by his imagination—a quite possible hypothesis.

In the descriptions given, Mr. O'Donnell is sometimes chased by one of these creatures, which will suddenly stop in its pursuit, a sign of the presence of the etheric double. It cannot go beyond a certain limit. But these are exceedingly terrifying creatures and apparently are very strong. It is for that reason that I am inclined to think that, if they exist, they may belong to the next class of beings, the "death-doomed bodies," the Mara Rupas, in whom the kamic principle is very strongly vivified, and rules the form. It does not seem credible that these lower creatures should have remained so long without the matter of their forms being dispersed, and therefore I think that, if they exist, they possibly belong to the Mara Rupa class. They are exceedingly dangerous, for they are animated always by undiscriminating hatred, and hatred of a very malignant kind.

It has always puzzled me why these seem to be the only inhabitants of the other world that Mr. O'Donnell has come across, and why others have not met them. Taking his accounts as true, it seems as if there must be something peculiar about his astral and etheric make-up, which has brought him so very much into contact with that kind of creature only. Happily he is a man of the most extraordinary courage, and by his will-power he has protected himself more than once; but according to his own account, he has been assaulted by these creatures in the most extraordinary way, and has come into a regular physical tussle with them, which is distinctly unpleasant. They are clearly not of the elemental kinds that we shall come to in a moment, which the human will is strong enough to drive away. There is some sort of brute consciousness in these creatures which does not make them so amenable to the ordinary human will.

CHAPTER XII

NON-PHYSICAL BEINGS: II

Then we come to the next class, the Mara Rupas, those who are doomed to death. These are the beings which include the "dwellers on the threshold" that H. P. Blavatsky has spoken of, and that you will find mentioned in Bulwer Lytton's book, *Zanoni*. These belong to particular persons, being their own cast-off astral bodies, vivified in the way now to be mentioned, and especially attracted to their former owners, as individuals, after they have reincarnated. In addition to these, the class includes all those whom H. P. Blavatsky called "soulless people," people who are on the down-grade, because the kamic body is so vitalized by the dragging away of the life which belongs to the lower part of the mental plane; this life has been so united with the molecular and atomic life in the astral bodies, that it is drawn downward; that is, part of the third life-wave is diverted and blended with the second life-wave. That will be the best way to think of it for the moment. Think of the third life-wave which gives man his individuality, and then think of the second life-wave which is the formative power in the building of bodies, and is essentially the life of the forms. That is a less developed form of life than is the third life-wave. Imagine that the third life-wave, which is animating the individual, has part of itself diverted and blended with the second; that is, that the life of the consciousness is blended with the life of the form. Remember that in that blending there is no obstacle, because they are both waves of the Divine Life; it is just like two streams of water coming together, and they mix as one stream. So with these two waves, which are both waves of the Divine Life, one more highly evolved for creative purposes than the other. If part of the higher is dragged away and blended with the lower, it lends to that lower life an enormously increased power.

So you have these forms and the imprisoned life of a now really sub-human being reincarnating, but on the downward path, each reincarnation being of a lower and lower type until it reaches the animal type, and so passes down, to be ultimately broken up, and re-used. These are what were called, in some of our earlier literature, the "three-principled" because the kama-manasic form comes in there. Some of the mind has been dragged away, and hence the increased vitality and the increased persistence. This marks off a distinct class which, like the "ghosts," sometimes come to the seance room, and show distinct malignity. The Mara Rupa is a far more intelligent being than the ghost, far more anxious to get hold of any available people, so as to feed upon them and intensify his life, which is always a fading quantity, which is always decreasing; so that you might imagine him as in a condition of perpetual hunger, always trying to get new nourishment, and hence he frequents those spiritualistic seances which have not been carefully guarded so as to shut out these lower beings.

We come next to the class that used to be called elementals; the class which in our later books we called elementaries—those with human forms. Those are a class which, if they are conscious on the astral plane, must be either of a very low type, or of a comparatively high one. The reason is this: if they are conscious in the astral body after death, it is usually because they are using its coarsest matter, and they are a very low type of human being—the savage, the murderer, the profligate, the drunkard—all those who strengthen the animal nature during their life-period on earth. All of those are in human forms; and those on the whole are they who are injured most if they are brought into touch with a medium. They want to remain in touch with the world because the whole of their desires are turned that way.

I think I told you once of a very unpleasant case that was observed in Paris by a doctor, who told me of it. He belonged to a little group of investigators who very rashly made arrangements with the French police department to hand over to them the bodies of criminals who had been guillotined. What they wanted was to find out whether it was possible to revive a person who had been guillotined. The plan was to replace the head immediately on the severed neck, so that the great blood-vessels were put together again before much time had elapsed; it was done by a special arrangement with the police. It has been found possible to get some signs of life in such a body by electric means; they succeeded in getting such a corpse to open its eyes, and to turn them in the direction of a person who spoke. Life did not remain, but they succeeded in getting such a brief revival.

The special point of which I wish to remind you is that they also carried on spiritualistic experiments in the room adjacent to the operating theatre, where these experiments on guillotined persons took place. On one occasion (which finished the seances there) a guillotined man turned up in his etheric double and astral body, and took possession of the medium, and a very severe fight took place between him and these unfortunate people; they escaped from the place, but this creature followed them down to the cab and tried to upset it—a very terrifying experience. That was a case showing the danger of a seance when carried on by people who do not know what they are doing; they were experimenters and materialists, and not occultists, and so they knew no way of guarding themselves from danger. There is that kind of danger also from others who have lately left the human physical body, and who are carrying on their life on the very lowest sub-planes of the astral.

It is a little perplexing to decide just what to include in the term "Asuras" when it is made to relate to astral world beings. In our later literature we have spoken of "Asuras" who came from one of the earlier planets and reincarnated here, beings of a very high condition of mentality and slight emotional development. They might be defined as astral beings having the forms of future men—on the way to human incarnation on this globe; that is their mark. Another class of astral beings are animal astral forms who are on the way upward. Those are now extremely rare, so far as incarnation in our humanity is concerned, but there are a few who will be human beings on this globe. Individualized animals pass into the astral world, but go onward into the mental, where they sleep, awaiting a world where human forms at a low stage of evolution are available. Animal elementals are very numerous in the astral, so far as the whole group is concerned of what are called animal devas, or "kama devas," by the Hindus —the devas of desire, who guide the animal kingdom.

These we usually speak of as "nature spirits," concerned with the animal kingdom, with the shaping and guiding of evolution among all the animals except the ants, birds, and one or two other classes who are on a separate line altogether. They are very interesting beings, moved, so far as their evolutionary work is concerned, by this impulsion which is embodied in them and which they cannot resist. They are apt to have a considerable amount of somewhat undefined intelligence; and by that I mean that it is not precise and accurate. For example, we are always thinking by differences; the moment you analyze your thought you will find that it is a process of noticing differences—you say: "It is not this, but it is that; A is not B," and so on. You are continually looking at the way in which a thing differs from other things, and your thought is a process of distinctions.

Now that is curiously absent in these kama devas. They see things more in groups by likenesses, and they do not distinguish differences in the same fashion. Their only way of looking at the world is to see the world in groups, groups of particular animals, groups of particular plants, groups of particular minerals, and so on. Everything is to them a general class, and the interdivisions of the class into smaller classes and individuals they do not seem to observe. They distinguish clearly between things that are hostile to their own group and things that are friendly. For instance, those who have to do with certain types of the various living creatures would distinguish between that group which is in their charge and the group of higher animals that prey upon them; they would distinguish between, for instance, the rabbits whose class is looked after by certain kama devas, and the weasel, the stoat, and other animals that live upon their particular charges, and are under other kama devas.

Further, they have the limited amount of intelligence which would make them color their creatures so as to avoid danger from those other classes. Suppose you take in the Arctic regions the animals of a certain class; you find that they become white in the time of snow, so that in running over the snow they may not stand out prominently to be seen by any enemy that might be about.

The protective colors and markings of all these creatures is one of the things that have been investigated to a considerable extent, as you will observe in some of the books on evolution, and those books are full of the most interesting cases of adaptation. The work of these devas is illuminative, because they explain, in a way which the ordinary book does not, the inner impulse which shapes the outer mechanism of the changes. You will find this especially so in the case of the adaptations which nature provides in the matter of the relations between the flower and the insect that is intended to fertilize it; both the proboscis of the insect and the protective sheath of the flower will become modified in consequence.

The whole of such changes, when they are regarded as purely mechanical, imply enormous ranges of time, because the changes are so exceedingly minute. But if you realize that behind these changes there is a little steady impulse going on, a little pressure, you then have exactly what seems to be lacking in the Darwinian theory. It is these kama devas which are pushing and pulling through the lower kingdoms, and so helping evolution on.

You will find the same thing with the National Devas. Although the great National Deva at the head of a Nation is, of course, of lofty intelligence, and is co-operating always with the Plan, that is not the case with the lower devas who belong to that same Nation. You will find them fighting on different sides in a battle-field. You will find the particular set of the lower German devas are fighting as much as they can for the Germans, while those on the side of the Allies are fighting on their side. That is going on all the time, and it is interesting to notice that as the intelligence grows in the higher and higher grades of these, more and more co-operation with the great Plan comes in, until you come to the highest National Deva, who is simply one of the lofty Intelligences working with the Hierarchy, working in perfect consciousness and deliberation into that Plan.

That principle was illustrated very clearly in the Russo-Japanese War, as preparing Russia for the part she is now playing and will play. The humiliation and defeat which she underwent were thoroughly acquiesced in by the Russian National Deva, who guided the people in that way for the sake of teaching them a lesson, and preparing them for the present part and for the future part which Russia will play in the coming evolution of Europe. There you get the conscious, deliberate working of the forces into the Plan.

In these lower stages, however, you find these devas quarrelling away as vividly as the people in physical forms are doing, just as the National heroes on both sides turn up and fight for their own people.

Another distinct class of astral beings are the Rakshasas, the astral forms of sorcerers. They are of very high mentality, but mentality of the rupa subplanes. Where the knowledge of the unity has been reached, even intellectually, there is a very strange change which occurs. In our old literature others were also spoken of who have reached a very, very high point of knowledge, but have reached it through the four lower sub-planes and are simply very highly developed mentally. There is a type, of very limited numbers, certainly, who, if included here, would come into the class of arupa, in whom the higher intellect is awakened with the intellectual recognition of unity. Those still remain tied by their past karma, but they have changed their motive. Recognizing the unity, they must recognize and do recognize that they have been on the wrong path, that it is not possible to materialize the world sufficiently (for evolution has gone too far) to hold it back and prevent it climbing on the upward arc. Under those conditions they have to work out the karma they have made, which is to work on the wrong side, that is, on the side of disintegration; but they work with a changed motive and endeavor to turn their forces against those who need strengthening by resistance in the spiritual life.

About the only person in the outer world who has caught sight of that is Marie Corelli; in her book on *Satan* she has touched on that point. It is not put there very well, but you will find in that the idea that I mean; the Satan there described is always glad when he is defeated. He exerts himself to oppose, but he rejoices when the man proves himself spiritual enough to resist, and at intervals he has a vision of the higher life.

That is a recognized side in the Hindu Puranas. There are many cases in which a man has evolved to a very high point of knowledge and then incarnates to expiate some of his past karma in the form of an opponent of good, like Ravana. There you have a being of this gigantic knowledge, who has gone through every form of experience which marks the gaining of great knowledge and power, but by his past karma is compelled to gather up in himself the evil forces of the world in order that they may be destroyed. Other religions have the same idea in different forms.

CHAPTER XIII

THE ROOTS OF DESIRE

You may recall that in a previous talk we observed that it is a person's own desires, his thirst for the objects of life, that bring him back to incarnation. You should realize this, so as to help the people who are beginning to think about reincarnation. When Western people first hear of reincarnation they always dislike it. "Oh, I have to come back here again!" —that is always the complaint; they do not want to come back, because there have been so many disagreeable things that have saddened them. They are tired of this life, and of course their being tired of it is a sign that the time is approaching for them to go on into another life.

A very large number of old people are very tired of this life. That tiredness controls the whole of their mentality, and they do not want to come back; they would much rather stay away. They would much rather look forward to a long rest in heaven. That idea is very prevalent; you may remember that it was expressed in the sentiment of one of the great French reformers who, when he was told that he was overworking and ought to rest, replied: "I have all eternity to rest in." His idea was somewhat muddled because, in the first place, he was in eternity then; in the second place, he did not have it to rest in. But that is the general idea, that you are going to rest for ever; very well then, overwork now; it does not matter.

That is a natural idea: the *body* is tired and, as the person identifies himself with the body, he is tired; clearly, then, he does not want to come back. And there is no reason why you should worry the poor person so much with the idea that he has to come back. First, help him to realize that he will not have to come back until he wants to do so, and you will find, if you try that plan, that it is a most consolling idea. If you say to a person: "You must come back," then he begins to protest; nobody likes a law that forces him to do what he does not want to do. He objects, and the more you press it on him the more angry he becomes. At the same time you are building up more and more obstacles in the way of his acceptance of the great law which you are trying to explain.

Do not argue with him on that line; you will never convince him. But say: "That is quite natural; of course you are tired; your body is worn out; you will not have to come back here until you want to do so." Then explain to him that nothing brings him back out of heaven except the getting tired of heaven and wanting to come back to earth—exactly the same feeling which now makes him want to escape from this world and go into heaven—and that he is entirely the master of his own destiny.

If you tell him that, you will find his objection disappears. Of course he will think that he never could get tired of heaven. That does not matter; he will get tired of it presently. Many people are already tired of the old conception that you find in the Bible

—the idea that they are going to stand around a throne of gold, and have a golden crown which they will put on and take off as occasion may determine. That is not by any means attractive to all, and not many people believe that now.

Uneducated people naturally like it; they are very poor, they are not used to gold, and what is nicer than to have a golden crown? What is nicer, inasmuch as it makes them happy, than to keep on singing "Hallelujah"? The very thought helps them through the present time; it is a symbol of the joy they will feel. And they will have exactly that when they go to the astral plane; they will have their golden crowns to take off and on, and the palms and the songs, for a very considerable time—in fact until they are tired of them, until they outgrow them.

If you think over it, it is a very wise arrangement for the whole of our worlds, that people go on doing the thing they like until they get tired of it; then they do not like it any longer; they have had enough of it. So, when you have once produced in the person a change of wish, you have done what is needed for his progress. Highly educated people often fail to realize what is meant by "the determination of the will." They say: "I can do as I like." The answer is: "Yes, you can do what you like; but the real problem is: What do you like, and what makes you like it?" That is, you take them a step further back.

Their feeling that they can do as they like is all right. They say: "If I want to walk to a door, and do so, I have free will." If they have the intelligence to follow your line of reasoning you can say: "But why do you want to go to the door; what has made you want to do that instead of walking to the window? Granted that you can do whatever you like, what makes you do one thing rather than the other? Either it is that you could go to the door and could not go to the window, or else that you preferred to go to the door and not to the window, to look at the landscape there." Then you ask: "What is it that makes you *want* to go to the door, or to do anything else?"

It is quite helpful that a person should thus keep on thinking backward in that way, in order that he may realize what it is that prompts him to want this thing or that. It is always better to get behind the immediate wish, because in that way you are able to introduce a new force which will help the persons to get a clearer conception of things.

It is that principle which is introduced in the lowest type of person, the animal-man, by punishment and the fear of punishment. It is that which is its justification at a certain low stage of evolution, even though people do not quite understand what is thus being done. What they are really doing, is to introduce the fear (a new force) of a certain result, which will determine the will against the particular line that it followed before. A man will not wish to rob another if he fears that it will result in imprisonment for himself.

It is just as well to remember that that is a true argument so far as it goes. You never will become really useful in the world in the molding of great changes, unless you are able to see what it is that supports the view that you are opposing. It is not any good merely to have your opinion, and to say that the other man is wrong. Unless you know why he is wrong from your standpoint, and give the full effect to that which has made his thought go in the line that you think wrong, you cannot change him.

That is the mistake that most people in the world make; they keep on reading always the things they agree with. Unless your thought is so weak that it needs additional arguments to support it, it is not wise to do what a person told me a few days ago he always did—go only to such lectures as he agreed with and not go to a single lecture against the thing that he believed. You should not listen to and read only the things you agree with. Of course, that may be very pleasant, for you may, perhaps, feel how clever you are to think the same things that these other people think. But it helps you only as long as you are not quite sure of your ground. Afterwards you should read the arguments on the other side, the things you do not agree with. That is the secret of power: read every book that you can get hold of, and listen to every person who is worth listening to, in order to see the thing that you do not agree with put in its best form. When you have got hold of the thing, with the reason behind it, you can begin to work on the persons who believe it. What you have to learn, as people who are trying to become Occultists, is: "Do not try to change what the man is doing, but what he is wishing to do."

You will then realize that to restrain a person by force from a particular kind of action is of very limited use. I do not say that it is of no use. People say that it is no good to prevent a man from doing a thing he wishes to do. That is not quite true, because a wish gets partly starved out by abstinence; and if a man is injuring himself and is in the grip of a bad habit he cannot break for himself, you may help him; that must not be forgotten. Many people get impatient over these considerations; they say it is impossible to balance all these different factors and know what is best.

We must therefore remember that at a certain stage a person can be helped by being prevented from doing the thing he wants to do, because a taste wears out by abstinence. If a man wants to get drunk, it is useful up to a certain stage to prevent him from getting drunk. But if you only prevent him from getting drunk, but do not touch the wish for physical gratification which lies behind the drunkenness, then, while you may destroy the taste for drink, you leave the craving behind it, and that will satisfy itself by some other physical relaxation, which may be as bad for him as the drink.

Take the same case when treated by hypnotism. H. P. B. considered it legitimate and even wise to lift a person out of drunkenness by hypnotism, provided you knew enough to be able to break the habit, and set free the will, so that it might set itself against the act of drinking. It is quite easy to cure a man of drinking by throwing him into a trance and by impressing upon him the idea: "Whenever you put a cup of drink to your lips, the moment you smell it, you shall be sick." That is the normal way of doing it, and that suggestion acts when the man has the drink before him. When he takes it up, the moment the odour reaches his nostrils he becomes violently sick. As that is not pleasant, he does not try it very often, and so he stops drinking. Where the drink habit is so strong and the man's will so weak that he cannot resist, hypnotism is a legitimate thing. But you must not think that hypnotism has done more than it has done. It has not cured him: it has only stopped a certain physical manifestation of a sensual desire, and if only that is done and the man is left alone, it has helped him very little. He at once falls into some other temptation, becomes a profligate, perhaps, which is even worse than drinking.

If by hypnotism you take the responsibility of breaking a bad habit by force, because the habit has paralyzed the man's will-power, the next thing to do is to devote yourself to that man's astral body, and help him there. Work upon the desire through the mind, which is the only way of curing a desire. Reason with him; if he will not listen to reason on the physical plane, reason with him when he is asleep, when you can reach him on the astral plane, and there put before him the reasons why he should not drink. That is, try to supply to the mind a motive behind the desire, which should be stronger than the desire and make him cease to desire to drink. Having freed the will, try to stimulate it through his own mind.

I have taken a very gross case in order to show you the method, but remember that it works with any other strong desire; it works in our own cases. We have first to consider what we wish: "What is it that I like?" That is the question you ought to ask yourself; it is what you like that shows your character. If it is something you ought not to like, and if you do not give way to it, that shows you are making a step forward. Inside you have recognized that you ought not to like it, and so you are trying to correct it. But as long as you like it you are in danger; any relaxation of the will, and you will do the thing you like. Your determination is good, you are beginning to stop the wrong desire; but that is not the end of your effort. You have to think over that liking, and to see into what part of your nature that liking has thrown down its roots, and so trace it out.

Next, take your mind. You can work directly upon the mind. You cannot work directly upon the liking, but you can work upon your thought, and think of the things which make that liking undesirable. There are two ways of getting rid of the liking; one is better than the other. The better way is to supercede the lower liking by a higher one, and so drop the lower—not fight against it.

That is the great value of devotion. You have some liking which you know is not quite good, and which would not be approved by somebody you love. Through your devotion to that person you make a strong effort to eliminate that liking, because you say to yourself: "So and So would not wish me to do this, would be sorry if he knew that I liked this." That is the better way, for that is the way of love, for thus your devotion is strong enough to substitute your wish to please that person for your wish to gratify something within you which you know is not the best side of your nature.

Sometimes a person cannot do it that way. Then he had better do it by the way of repulsion. Suppose a person has a craving for drink or for sexual gratification. He may get rid of it either by the way I have just described, or by the method that is sometimes used i yoga. The man is set to work this out mentally and deliberately to its inevitable physical consequences. He is told to think of the results of drinking, beginning with its effect upon him. He thinks of what happens the morning after his debauch; how he wakes up with a bad headache, his mouth feels uncomfortable, and so on through all the physical symptoms which he can get rid of only by drinking again. When he is not intoxicated, he thinks all this out and imagines it as vividly as he can. He then goes on down the line of the degradation of the drunkard: the gradual nervous degeneration, the shaking of the hands, the confusion of the thought, and all the rest of it, until he traces himself down and down and down to the condition of *delirium tremens*, strongly imagining himself living through those stages. In the normal man, if you can persuade him to do that, it will induce such a revulsion that he will leave off drinking.

You ought to state also the results on the other side of death, if he believes in the post mortem life, and trace out for him in picture what happens in the astral world under these conditions of drink. I have cured an inveterate drunkard in that way by producing in him such a terror of the results that he gave it up. He thought that he would have to go through this frightful career, which was quite true if he continued drinking, and from fear of it he gave up drinking. In one case where that result was produced, it lasted for some years. The man was a Prince, and he might have gone on cured, had he not foolishly yielded to the solicitations of his courtiers, as a result of which he died of *delirium tremens* and had to face the drunkard's fate on the astral plane.

You can do the same with the sexual impulse. You set yourself every day to think of its results: that it brings about nervous degeneration in the same way; that the will becomes paralyzed, the nerves get weak, and then weaker and weaker until they get beyond cure; and finally the person becomes a wreck. Also one adds how, if that be persisted in, there is very great suffering on the other side of death. Unless a man is an absolute fool, that will help him; but if he is an absolute fool, then he must go through it and bear the results. This is not the better method, as I said, but it is preferable to continuing a victim of undesirable habits.

That is the value in what is called "punishment," in making a man suffer. If it is self-inflicted, it is legitimate. Personally I do not think that any form of punishment is legitimate with a grown-up person, except that of sufficient physical restraint to prevent him from injuring another person; that would be the only exception. If a man is violent or a murderer, you have a right to prevent him from hurting or murdering another person; but I do not think you have the right to make his life miserable. But that is going very far, and it is only my own view. I believe we have the right, collectively, through society, to restrain him or to exile him, but not to punish him further.

I do not believe in punishment in the case of a child because the child is so plastic that you can influence him by love, if you have enough love within you to do it. But a stage comes when the human being has passed beyond the plasticity of childhood, and when you must have an external restraint to prevent him from injuring others. There I think society has a right to lock him up; he is a form of maniac, and we cannot have people murdered by allowing this man to exercise his distorted free will.

In the old days that was one advantage of exile. If they had criminals who were so much below the level of the civilization of the place where they lived that they would not submit to the laws of the place, they did not punish them; they simply sent them out of the country. They said: "All right, go where you will be more comfortable; and we shall be more comfortable without you." That is a legitimate position for a State to take; but that is very, very far from the position taken nowadays.

The main point that I wish to emphasize for the moment is that there is a certain justification in the minds of the people who favor the employment of violent methods of punishment, and that you should understand that before you argue with them. If you argue with them fairly, you may convince them that yours is the better attitude, but if you argue with them unfairly, you will only confirm them in their ideas.

That is why I ask you, who are learning to be occultists, to go to the root of all things. We have often said to you that occult training is not in teaching but in life; you have to learn life and understand the hidden forces that are playing in all departments of it. If you can do that, you have become an occultist, even though you may know nothing about Rounds and Races and all the rest of the things that you read in books. An occultist does not become one by reading books, but by living, and you might meet a very fine occultist who did not possess the smallest idea of Rounds and Races. That is all, so to speak, trivial; it is very interesting and useful, but is not of the essence of the occult life.

All of you who want to be of service when the Lord Maitreya comes, must try to learn the deeper principles that underlie the occult life; they are the principles that Theosophy teaches with their application to everyday events, and it is those things that you should really learn; but it will be only by your own application of the principles, and not so long as they are only hearsay to you. If you will only apply them to yourself and to the assistance of those who are in trouble around you, it will help you and them. And I hope you will do this before the Lord comes, because then you will be much more useful.

That is the way we are looking at our present work: not "Are we gaining in knowledge?" but "Are we more useful?" That is the only thing that matters just now, and that is the only thing that is of value to those who come to Adyar to-day. It is not a bit of good coming here only for what you hear said at our various meetings, except so far as you practice it. Knowledge is useful only if it helps you to live and to serve.

CHAPTER XIV

THE REALITY OF DEVACHAN

One of the greatest difficulties in the study of an abstruse subject, removed from the daily life of the people, is the conveying of new ideas in an old language, a language which has no words for the ideas, for the simple reason that the ideas themselves have not reached the mind. The difficulty is, of course, met in every science, for every science has its own terminology. A single word expresses a botanical fact, and unless the word is mastered the fact will demand a descriptive sentence. When the Physical Research Society burst on an astonished world, it found itself face to face with many facts, never before recognized in the West, and it consequently created for itself a considerable number of hitherto unknown words, through which new facts, and new relationships between facts, were definitely brought to the notice of the bewildered and impatient world.

Theosophy has much the same experience, but it was able, more or less, to shelter itself under the use of Sanskrit words, familiar at least to scholars. After a time we sought and found English equivalents, often at the cost of accuracy and sharp-cut lucidity, and contented ourselves with conveying as much of the ideas as we could in familiar, everyday English.

But far more difficult is the work, when the idea presented to the western student is wholly alien from his habits of thought. This criterion of reality is objectivity—"I thought that; I imagined that; I only fancied that." If you tell him that the products of his thought, of his imagination, of his fancy, are far more "real" than the chairs and tables round him, he becomes confused, bewildered. Hence to him Devachan is unreal; it is a dream, it is a creation of his fancy, it is sheer waste of time to dwell in that "fool's paradise." Nothing can be more outrageously mistaken. The Spirit, who is Man, clothes himself in matter, as he descends through world after world. He clothes himself in Buddhic matter, and shuts out some of the Reality which he contacted at every point in the Nirvanic world. He draws round himself a cloak of mental matter, and shuts out more of his splendid heritage of far-reaching life and power. More still vanishes from his ken as he envelops himself in the denser matter of the lower mental world, and still more as he dons his cloak of astral matter, finally entering the narrow limits of his physical prison-house. The crude and heavy contacts of these coarser forms of matter seem to him to be more real—because less amenable to his control—than the potent work of his subtler forces when they shape and mould the luminous matter of the higher worlds. He does not realize that the forms he creates in the higher mental worlds are full of vitality, full of shaping power, and that they generate a thousand thought-forms which enter human brains and result in physical events. The "dreams" of Devachan create the thoughts, and the thoughts of prophets create the thought-forms that fill the atmosphere in which men live and move. These thought-forms stimulate receptive human brains and stir them into action, and then men see coming forth great reforms, religious, social, political, which would not have come into being in the lower world had it not been for the dreamer in Devachan.

How many of our thoughts are mere fragments, a glimpse, a momentary aspiration, a scarce-formulated hope! But in Devachan, the dreamer stays himself on the glimpsed fragment, and patiently works it out in every detail, in every possibility of splendid performance; he builds it, shapes it, molds it, in all its variegated possibilities, and tosses it out into the world of form; there every dream-germ in it burgeons into fullness and beauty, and the popularizers of ideals pick it up, and gloat over it, and worship it, until their whole being is transfused with its beauty; and then they hold it up before the eyes of men, and it becomes a mighty inspiration, put into schemes of reform, into philanthropic agencies, into political proposals, into a myriad forms that blossom in the desert of the world and turn it into a garden, the Garden of Allah. When some eager enquirer follows the trail backward, he comes at last to the solitary dreamer, out of whose radiant thought-stuff the whole wonderful changes have been woven, who in his useless dreaming has recreated a world.

This marvelous power of thought-creation is a familiar idea in the East, but its practice is not as common as its theory. The ordinary man who would create by thought, as he sits silent, too often passes into a state of mere vacuity, or goes to sleep. Creation by thought implies sustained concentration, one of the most difficult of achievments, and one of the most fatiguing withal. Years of practice go to the making of the creative thinker, and more than one life is devoted to his building. Not by the careless, the idle and the frivolous may these heights of God-head be gained.

This is but one example of the difficulty experienced by Western students in grasping Eastern ideas. To the Westerner all that is non-physical is nonreal; to the Easterner the physical is the farthest removed from reality. Reality is the Eternal; when the Eternal manifests in space and time, each limit of space, each limit of time superposed thereon, piles unreality on unreality; each limit removed brings us nearer to reality. To the Westerner Nirvana is annihilation, nothingness, emptiness; to the Easterner it is that on which all lesser things depend for their limited existences. "Nirvana is," said the Lord Buddha; but even He could not explain it within the limits of human language. He stated that all was dependent on it, that without that uncreated, the created could not be, but even He could not say what Nirvana is; He could only assert, "It is;" there silence falls. But those who by way of meditation have risen beyond the physical, and have experienced the extension of consciousness which follows the falling away of physical bonds; those who have risen beyond the astral world, and have passed onward into worlds of ever subtler and less resistant matter; those who have found that with each rising into subtler worlds, life becomes more vivid and intense, intellect more far-reaching, emotion more exquisite, power more compelling, the Self more gloriously realized—those can dimly conceive ranges that stretch beyond them of ever-increasing possibilities, "dark with excess of light."

Thus looked at, Devachan becomes a world two degrees nearer to reality than is the physical world; it is essentially a world of causes, on which our next life in the physical world depends. Thither we carry the raw materials we have gathered in the physical world, the mental and emotional experiences which forward our evolution, and there we weave them into the character with which we return to earth; there also we work out our aspirations into detailed plans ready for achievement on our return, so that the physical world may evolve; there we are creators, and our creations are clothed in dense matter down here.

Moreover that creative work does not await our return to earth. As we create, the embryos of the future are conceived in the womb of physical time and space; there they grow in the silence and the darkness, living germs continuously nourished by our thought, until they fully reproduce the completed ideal of their creator. Forces are set going in the lower world which prepare the way; brains of prophets, of poets, of thinkers, catch gleams of our thoughts, and prepare less sensitive brains for their partial reception. Thus the forces which make for evolution work from above, and press the world ever onward and upward; and when we are reborn into the physical world, blinded by the grosser matter which envelops us, we work in ignorance along the lines we laid down in knowledge, as our hands now work out unconsciously the idea which the controlling brain impels them to construct. Our brain is the organ of our mind in Devachan, and we in the physical world are its hands.

The analogy is true in many ways. The hands do not understand the brain, although they obey its orders, but the brain understands the hands. The hands do not look before and after, but the brain imagines and remembers. Men down here may not realize how limited is their physical consciousness, and that they are living in more worlds than one. But only a very small portion of their consciousness is submerged in the physical world, though, in that physical world, they can only know the things of which that part of their consciousness is aware. Hence the "unreality" to them of the things which are nearer to reality in the other worlds which surround and interpenetrate the physical, as the senses are unconscious of the surrounding and interpenetrating ether, though we live and move in it continuously and it forms part of our very bodies; to the senses the ether is unreal, being invisible, inaudible, intangible, without taste or smell. To the ear, color is unreal; to the eye, music is unreal. Everywhere we find limitations, and our very senses are merely the windows created by our will to come in contact with the physical world. It is the Self that wills, and creates the organs in each world of matter by which his will fulfills itself. Thus have we learned.

Because of the difference of viewpoint, the Mystic has always seemed to be an unpractical dreamer to the "man of the world." Yet is the man of one world only the unconscious agent of his mystic Self, the blind, deaf hand working under the impulses of his own Self, whom he denies. It is he who is the dreamer immersed in the fog of illusions, not seeing his way, groping along through the fog, thinking lamp-posts to be living enemies, and transforming things familiar in the light into menacing, strange, unfamiliar shapes looming through the darkness. When the fog clears away he becomes the Mystic since the Mystic is only the man in the daylight who sees things in their own shapes, and in true proportions and relations.

All this seems queer and unreal to the ordinary Westerner, but it only seems queer and unreal because it is unfamiliar. Taking this physical world as the real world, with some vague, indefinite "heaven" beyond it, how can the "practical man" explain the things going on around him to-day? How can he explain the War, in which millions of men are being killed, mutilated, their lives, if they survive, rendered a burden to them? How can he explain the maimed future of the Nations, deprived of the flower of their youth, of their best, their bravest, their most self-sacrificing, rent away from them? How can he explain the ghastly disproportion of the sexes that will reveal itself after the War, how answer the problems of re-population, of the necessary motherhood combined with the necessary production of all that is needed in civilized life? Is not this welter of blood and pain unintelligible, horrible, maddening, unless brotherhood, reincarnation, karma and sacrifice are seen as the laws of life, and their recognition as laws of nature is seen as the condition of happy and peaceful human life, in society as well as in the individual? If reincarnation be a natural law and the condition of evolution, then the tremendous slaughter of the battle-field becomes a negligible incident in its ultimate effects, and it is a dramatic forcing on the attention of the Nations of the fact that this loss of human life is less than is annually caused by the neglect of the law of brotherhood, a neglect causing a huge infantile mortality, an underfeeding and ill-housing of masses of the population, bringing about conditions of low vitality and of premature death that are avoidable, and therefore criminal. If the law of sacrifice be true, then the voluntary sacrifice by the manhood of the Nations of all that makes life fair, by the womanhood of the Nations of all that makes life happy, must result in a leap forward in evolution that will bring them swiftly to earth again to build up a nobler civilization, that will turn its back on war—whether of Nations or of classes—will substitute law for force, and brotherly co-operation for contest. The War has substituted the willing sacrifice of earthly life by millions for the enforced sacrifice of that life by millions through social injustice. The latter sacrifice brought increased National degradation; the former will bring life from the dead. The recognition of the law of karma will enable men to plan for the future with the certainty of the results aimed at, substituting the inviolability of law for chance happenings in daily life. Life will become a science, instead of a gamble.

The War will thus become merely a swift and certain way of accomplishing in a few years the work of centuries, of insuring an unexampled progress toward a nobler and better civilization.

To us, who are among those who see also in the War the clearing away of many hoary forms of evil, the destruction of otherwise irremovable obstacles in the way of the Coming of a World-Teacher, who will lay the foundations of the New Age, and give a fresh impulse of life and of happiness to a weary and outworn world—to us, necessarily, the War is but a presage of His Coming, a sign that the world's Salvation is drawing nigh. We look around us, and as when the bonds of icy winter are on the world in western climes, but the coming of spring is heralded by the movement of the sap in the trees, the swelling of buds that shall be the leaves of summer, and perchance the pushing of a snowdrop through the earth, that rings its tiny bell of white petals in the winter air, rivalling the white snow which it pierces, so is it now with us. Still in the bitter cold of the winter, we presage the coming of the spring; we see its signs, we feel its breath, and we faintly hear in the distance the footfalls of the coming Lord. To us, at least, the words prove true: "Let not your heart be troubled, neither let it be afraid."

CHAPTER XV

A THOUGHT-WORLD

One of the greatest difficulties in the way of Western students is a realization of Devachanic conditions; this is partly due to their habit of connecting reality with physical phenomena, and regarding as unreal the phenomena of worlds higher than the physical. The very terms used, "subjective" and "objective," imply "imagination" in the first and reality in the second. That the creations of the imagination are more real than the creations of the hands is a novel, and hence an unwelcome, view of life. That an idea is more real than a club, sounds absurd to the ordinary Westerner. That the results flowing from the first category are more vital, more vivid, more beneficent or destructive, and are objective phenomena in their own world, and far more widespread in their effects in the lower worlds than those of the second category, appears to the man in the street a topsy-turvy view of life. So seemed to him wireless telegraphy until his physical ear at the receiver heard the message.

Now the Eastern student starts from the opposite pole of thought. To him the real is the unseen, the eternal, and every veil of matter in which this unseen and eternal Reality is clothed, causing external separateness, intuition, mentality, emotion, physical embodiments, in a descending series, is one more stage of unreality imposed upon the Real. He is like a man who understands that over his eyes are placed a series of distorting glasses, each one increasing the distortion of his external surroundings and also dimming their clearness. He sees the outer world, but he sees it wrongly, distorted and dimmed; but he knows that he is seeing it thus, and that it is unreal as he sees it, while the average man, though looking at his surroundings through such distorting and dimming glasses of matter, does not know that it is unreal as he sees it, and that its real appearance from the centre is quite different from the appearance that he sees.

Try for a moment to imagine yourself as without a physical body, clothed only in your astral body and bodies composed of yet finer matter; if then I hit you with a club, you would not feel it, the club would pass through you, it would not knock you down; you could walk through this table; you could sit down on this chair, and another of us seeing the chair apparently empty could sit down on the chair through you. You could walk through the rest of the class, and its members could walk through you. You could enter through the closed door, or come down through the ceiling, or come up through the floor, and leave the room in similar fashion. All the ordinary tests of reality would fail you under these conditions, and the physical world would to you be unreal, non-objective, a world of dream to you, when living in your astral body, intangible, and one which you could not act upon directly, in which you could not create objects nor destroy them, a world which you could neither effect nor be effected by—an unreal world.

When Theosophy appeared in the western world, this was at its nadir of spirituality, its zenith of materialism. Psycho-physiology was making its way, beginning in resolute materialism. To it, the workings of consciousness were regarded—especially by the leaders of science in Germany—as the product of certain arrangements of nervous matter; Karl Vogt's trenchant phrase was often quoted: "The brain secretes thought as the liver secretes bile." If it were suggested that thought was not, like bile, a chemical product but an immaterial thing of a different order, the answer came that in a cell made of physical matter you could, by a certain arrangement, generate a galvanic force, and that thought was a force, not yet well investigated, which might well be produced by chemical reactions in the brain. Thought might be a resultant of physical and chemical action, and a whole series of exquisitely careful experiments was devised to investigate the travelling of waves in nervous matter, appearing as sensations when they reached the brain.

Inevitably these investigations—like all honest and patient efforts to understand Nature—led the investigators toward truth, in this case into the borderland which separates the physical from the superphysical worlds. The Spiritualists had long been colonizing it with the help of the mediums, and had tabulated many of its phenomena; men like Sir William Crookes, Stainton Moses, and Richet had been carrying on careful investigations and obtained remarkable results. The Psycical Research Society had collected an immense number of observations and had made many carefully devised and accurately recorded experiments, proving to all students that the materialistic basis of science was inadequate as an explanation of the observed facts of Nature. The Theosophical Society showed, in the person of some of its members, that human evolution might be quickened, and that it was not necessary to await the sporadic "sports" of unassisted Nature in producing clairvoyants, clairaudients, and other exceptional people, who could explore the subtler worlds and report their observations, but that such people could be produced by a course of training along the lines of the ancient eastern science of yoga. The result of all this was the definite recognition by Western psychologists of the "dream-consciousness," functioning beyond the "waking," as a subject for careful investigation, no longer one for ridicule as superstition, nor for reprobation as wicked. Gradually the view triumphed that, so far from matter being the fount and origin of life, life was the shaper and molder of matter. Eastern phsychology traced back both matter and life to the "One, without a second," and saw in them the dual manifestation of the Unmanifested Unity. Western science, with Haeckel as its prophet, taught Monism, with matter as the prolific source of all; Eastern science, with Rishis as its Teachers, also taught Monism, but Monism with an Unmanifested One as the Fount of a Dual Manifestation found throughout the universe, which man studies.

It will be readily understood that to minds steeped in the ideas drawn from a materialistic science, Eastern ideas were too revolutionary to be readily accepted. Fortunately, one of the Rishis—whom we call "Masters"—responsible for the Theosophical Society, had as one of pupils Mr. A. P. Sinnett, then editor of the Pioneer, a man who was himself steeped in the scientific thought of the time, and who had as his intimate friend Sir—then Mr.—William Crookes; he was well versed in the latter's researches into post-mortem existence, and was also without the hide-bound prejudice of Mr. Crookes's colleagues which nearly lost the most eminent physicist and chemist of his day his well-earned place in the Royal Society. Mr. Crookes—I may remind you in passing—with his rare intuition, welcomed the old-new Light of Theosophy, and was one of the earliest members of the Theosophical London Lodge, of which Mr. Sinnett was the honored President.

Before Mr. Sinnett's eyes, the great Indian Rishi unrolled the vast panorama of a sevenfold universe, with its five planes of human evolution, and, through our revered and beloved H. P. Blavatsky, He precipitated most of the letters written about in Mr. Sinnett's revealing book, *The Occult World,* the letters which formed the basis of *Esoteric Buddhism;* his scientific training, with occult teaching superimposed upon it, made him exactly the messenger fitted to carry Theosophical truth to the then materialistic western world; and if the pretty Christian idea be true, that every soul "saved" by the truth brought to him by a teacher forms a star in that teacher's heavenly crown, then Mr. Sinnett would need a hundred heads to carry all the crowns, each gemmed with innumerable stars, representing the souls whom he has illuminated.

Owing, however, to the deeply ingrained western habit of looking at life from the circumference instead of from the centre, all of us who wrote in England on Devachan, the heavenly world, unconsciously represented it as a dream-world, a world of thought—as indeed it is—without understanding that it was nearer to reality, not farther from it, by the dropping of the two distorting glasses of the physical and astral bodies, and that this so-called "subjective state" was filled with far more vivid experiences than the so-called "objective," and might be utilized far more than the physical for the quickening of our evolutionare pace. Not understanding this, and misled by the supposed connotations of eastern terms, such as were translated "illusion." "unreal," and the like, we regarded the time spent in Devachan as "wasted," and were wont to say: "I don't want to go to Devachan."

If we had considered the great difference between the relative lengths of the periods passed in the physical and mental worlds respectively, we might have reached a more rational view than the one we then took of Devachan. We might have realized that the Divine Wisdom, which planned human evolution, would scarcely have set apart a century or less for the useful part of the life-period, and many centuries for the useless. We might have considered that in the dawn of consciousness in the animal man and during its infancy in the savage, incarnation after incarnation succeeded each other very swiftly, and that what interval there was was spent on the astral plane with a mere touch with the devachanic, and that the devachanic period lengthened as the mind developed, until in the advanced stage, before actual initiated discipleship, when fresh influences are at work, the periods spent in Devachan became longer and the growth in successive earth-lives was far more strongly marked.

"Progress," once said a Master, "is arithmetical in the lower stages, geometrical in the higher." Why should this be, and why should it be accompanied by such different lengths of time in Devachan, if the periods spent there were practically wasted?

The general truth is that in the physical world the man gathers experience; in the devachanic world he works out that experience into every possibility contained in it as a germ of thought. The germ is taken and the mind evolves it into a mighty tree of capacity, and of activities springing out of that capacity; these are all lived through with a vividness that nothing on earth can rival; any experience passed through in the body is dull, colorless, lifeless, as compared with the springing, glorious, many-colored radiance of that intense ecstasy of the very essence of life, that marks those of Devachan. It must be remembered that happiness, joy, promote all life-energies, and where happiness is deepest and most radiant there the whole nature expands and grows. What then of the growth in that perfect joy of Devachan, where no sorrow can intrude to cloud, no pain to mar?

Think of choosing a single idea, of following it out into all its branching byways, into all the suggestions it throws out, each of these also to be followed out similarly; think of each idea in the long succession as being an object to the thinker—for he is in a world of thought, where every thought is a living form, where there is nothing else but thoughts, for there is no matter, except mental matter—thought-stuff, as Clifford called it. In that world are solids and liquids and gases, of varying density, and color, and consistency, and quality. There is no sense of dream nor of unreality, but thronging, joyous realities, visible, audible, tangible, exquisite—all shaped out of thought-stuff, less distorting the life within them than that same life is distorted down here by its additional vestures of astral and physical matter.

None of us realizes how our thoughts in this physical world are creating our karma, since in thought lies our creative power. Each thought creates a line of thoughts which grow out of it, and these again branch out; desires and actions clothe the thought-forms, so that these make or mar our future lives. This intricate network of our thoughts enmeshes those future lives, and is the cause of the great complexity of the threads of our destinies. Hence the difficulty of tracing an event to its karmic causes, indefinitely numerous, and the difficulty found by students, when a series of the lives of an individual is placed in their hands in tracing the connections between them. Broad lines of karma stand out, the trend of evolution, the relationship between groups of people, the friendships and the enmities which come down through the ages. We can see enough for encouragement and for warning, but not for anything approaching full understanding. The lives are like a mosaic, rather than a connected growth. And why? Because the observers record actions and not thoughts, the finished result and not the causes which brought it to the surface. If the observer concentrated his attention on the thoughts of the individual observed, and traced out each thought as it worked itself out in Devachan, volumes would be required for narrating a single life. That life in Devachan would be the immense field of study. As we merely glimpse the complexity, the intricacy, the outstretching lines passing beyond our vision, we dimly feel that only the Lipika, the Lords of Karma, living in Nirvana, can suffice for the tremendous task of applying the karmic law. If we try to follow out the byways starting from a single thought and their results, and then remember that the devachani does this with every thought in his recent life on earth, we realize the hopeless impossibility, at our present stage of evolution, of grasping the totality of karmic causes in the life of any individual. We can see that in the case of a person who owes a karmic debt to another person. the two must be brought together in some physical life, and that this fact may hold over the payment for many lives. Many similar instances may be noted, sufficient to establish the great principles of karma, but in the application of those principles to particular cases we have not data sufficient to guide us to a definite conclusion.

The fact that karmic debts may be left over, owing to the impossibility of bringing debtor and creditor together, thus affording the opportunity of payment, sometimes results in very curious apparent contradictions. A poet spoke of the Chancellor, Bacon, as the "greatest, wisest, meanest, of mankind." The collocation of greatness, wisdom and meaness is obviously impossible, and no one who recognizes the greatness of that extraordinary man can, for one moment, believe that he stooped to the acts debited to him. Here is a case where a splendidly unfolded Spirit had incurred debts in a long-past incarnation that remained undischarged, and that had to be paid to the uttermost farthing before he could cross the threshold of Liberation. His supreme greatness and supreme wisdom, as measured with men, could not relieve him from his ancient, undischarged liabilities, incurred, perchance, when he was neither great nor wise. A man who would become a Jivanmukta, a liberated Spirit, must, as he approaches the threshold, sweep out all the corners of his longpast lives, with their forgotten fragments of ancient enmities, of ancient evil done, and burn them to ashes on the fire of suffering. As he cannot at the stage he has reached do the ills that would entail bitter reproach on him, false accusations must be brought against him, convincing proofs must smirch his reputation, scandal must launch at him its poisonous darts. Why should Bacon escape the fate of his peers? Nay, was not the very Christ accused of treason to his Emperor, was He not betrayed by His disciple, mocked and jeered at by the populace, slain as a malefactor, He the emblem and the type of all the Crucified, ere they can rise to be the Saviours of the world? Therefore has the way of Liberation been called for immemorial ages the Way of the Cross. Every Christ must be crucified, must be "made perfect through suffering," must thus attain the stature of the Perfect Man, of Man become God.

But the world cannot see men in this fashion, nor recognize its Christs. Its crude and hasty judgments and condemnations are also useful in evolution. Its standard is about as high as average persons can appreciate, and its wide-flung aspersions have in them this of uplift, that the condemnation of the vice is good for it, even if the particular person assailed be not guilty of the sin. "Righteous indignation" has its place at a certain stage of evolution, where the feeling of strong repulsion is necessary to keep the recent sinner—my "recent" may cover lives—from falling back again into the mire whence he has emerged. "To understand all is to forgive all," and is also the condition of giving a judgment which is just. But a wide tolerance is not always wholesome in its effects, if shown too publicly, for it is difficult to make people in general understand that the absence of condemnation is not necessarily due to moral indifference. The conditions of evolution stretch over such huge periods of time that they cannot be available as data for judgment until a person has himself reached a certain point; a man must have climbed to a certain height upon the mountain side, before he can see over the plains. Hence the wisdom of the direction: "Judge not."

PEACE TO ALL BEINGS.